LEADERSHIP BEYOND THE JOB

30 Ways for Older Teens and Young Adults to Develop Effective Leadership Skills

ISRAELIN SHOCKNESS

Successful Youth Living - Vol. 1

VANQUEST PUBLISHING

motivating | inspiring | educating

Cataloguing-in-Publication Data

Israelin Shockness

Includes bibliographical references.

LEADERSHIP BEYOND THE JOB

30 Ways for Older Teens and Young Adults to Develop Effective Leadership Skills

ISBN: 978-1-989480-01-4 (Paperback)

ISBN: 978-1-989480-00-7 (Ebook)

SERIES- Successful Youth Living - Vol. 1

DISCLAIMER

All materials provided in this book are for informational purposes only and should not be taken as a substitute for professional, psychological, or mental health advice. These materials are intended to encourage and motivate readers to think and to have meaningful conversations around the issues discussed, the objective being to promote more responsible behavior at all times. If, for any reason, a reader may be experiencing any emotional or other crisis, that reader is encouraged to seek out professional care. References have been made to peer-reviewed and other research studies and works, but this is not intended to imply specific endorsement of this author's work by any of these authors and professionals mentioned. Any incorrect attribution of ideas to an author was not intentional and will be corrected at earliest possibility. The opinions expressed in this book are solely those of this author and not those of the publisher. Further, the publisher is exempt from any responsibility for actions taken by readers with respect to the content. The publisher also acknowledges that readers act of their own accord in using information presented and hold the author and the publisher blameless in the readers' use of the content.

PURPOSE OF THIS SERIES

Successful Youth Living is a series of books, dealing with issues, which older teens and young adults face as they go through the uncertainty of adolescence. A few of the topics dealt with are: becoming a leader in your own right without being a bully; learning how to assume responsibility; fostering positive attitudes and habits for self-growth; learning how to continue your education regardless of where you stopped or whether you dropped out; developing emotional intelligence and caring for self and others; learning how to deal with stress; recognizing the importance of personal reflection; and being a person that others admire for the right reasons.

The 'seed' for these volumes was actually planted when the author, then a teenager on a scholarship, almost dropped out of university because of issues that had nothing to do with school. Thanks to the insightfulness and mentorship of a professor, the author became a teen mentor, committing herself to helping vulnerable teens and young adults from losing their way, the way she had almost lost hers.

After years of further study, a career as an educator working with children, teens and young adults, years as a volunteer in marginalized communities and as a columnist in a weekly community newspaper, Israelin has recognized that many of the issues plaguing adolescents have not changed. She has therefore decided to share ideas she has gleaned over the years, with the hope that these ideas would be a catalyst for thinking and discussion among teens and young adults, preparing them for making split-minute decisions that they may have to make in the future.

DEDICATION

I dedicate this book to all those young people, and older ones too, who aspire to be good leaders. Whether you see yourself as an adolescent, a teenager, an emerging adult, a youngster, a young adult, or a young millennial, this book is for you. If you are a parent, grandparent, friend, family member, or an adult working with younger people, this book is also for you, because you can make sure that the younger people in your lives have the opportunity to reflect on the issues dealt with in this book. You may also find the book a good read that you could pass on to a young person. Now, words to the young person.

WORDS TO THE YOUNG PERSON

As a young person, just starting out on life's journey, you have the opportunity to be intentional about the kind of person you want to be and the kind of leadership you want to provide to others. It means living your life as an example to those who look up to you: your siblings, your family members, your friends, and the other people whose lives cross paths with yours. At the same time, it means looking to mentors that could lead you in best practices.

I have been fortunate to have had mentors throughout my life, mostly older people, whose wisdom has been unfathomable, and whose generosity has been a blessing. I have also learned from younger people, true leaders in their own right, who had fresh eyes for old problems and who shared their ideas with me. Then, there are the many outstanding examples of good leaders whom I have only known from afar and whose lives and works will continue to be a living legacy that I will share with others.

LEARN TO BECOME A GOOD EXAMPLE

Therefore, first and foremost, as a leader, you have to learn to become a good example. As Jack Welch, a former Chairman and CEO of General Electric, who was responsible for the phenomenal growth at this organization, noted: "Before you are a leader, success is all about growing yourself. When you become a leader, success is all about growing others."

John F. Kennedy, former president of the United States, noted: "Leadership and learning are indispensable to each other." Brian Tracy, motivational speaker, noted: "Become the kind of leader that people would follow voluntarily, even if you had no title or position." Ralph Waldo Emerson, 19th century American poet, maintained: "Our chief want is someone who would inspire us to be what we know we could be."

IMPORTANCE OF LEARNING AND DEVELOPING

What all of these have pointed out is the importance of learning and developing to be all that you can be and through your example encouraging others to grow as well and be all that they can be. Becoming a leader has to be intentional, with you making the decision to acquire the habits and ways of behaving that identify you as a leader, whether or not you have a job that says you are. This is because leadership is not about bossing other people around, but rather about influencing others to be the best people they can be.

In the twenty-first century, many of our world leaders have let us down. Many have failed us miserably. This is the time when we should all be asking the difficult question: Who or what is a good leader? The answer we should take away from this deficit in leadership is that it is time we should all learn about true leadership.

FOCUS FOR THE YOUNG

Learning about leadership is about looking at people that you admire because they possess good character, discipline, good behaviour, respect, honour, and fair play, who are kind, upright, people of integrity, and who care about others as they care about themselves. It was Ray Kroc, American businessman, who was credited with turning McDonald's into the most successful fast-food restaurant in the world, and who was quoted as saying, "The quality of a leader is reflected in the standards they set for themselves." Be a great leader and set high standards for yourself.

Our older adults are depending on you, young people, to become the true leaders in our society. Take up the mantle of good leadership and ignore what now passes for leadership.

With the world before you and opportunities around you, be the leaders you can be proud to be today and in the future. Where there may not be opportunities, make them. Use these chapters as a basis for thinking about ways you can "grow yourselves" to be the truly great leaders that you can be and that our world deserves.

And as you read, think of your many friends, family members, classmates or work mates with whom you can share some of these ideas. Think about the many peers who can also "grow themselves" and be truly great leaders as you can be. Maybe you are already a leader and you are recognized as one. Then use your leadership skills to help other young people to become even better leaders.

TABLE OF CONTENTS

CHAPTER 1

CHOOSING YOUR ROLE MODEL

Many leaders today would confess that as they were growing up, certain people had great impact on their lives. It may have been a parent, a coach, a teacher, a professional athlete, a celebrity, or just someone they may have admired. Sometimes the admiration comes from having a close relationship with that person, but sometimes the admiration may be from a distance, or even from a stranger's autobiography. These admired individuals serve as leaders or role models.

But does everyone have a role model? To some degree, people have others they admire and that they aspire to be like. Sometimes, the process is quite unconscious.

My own role model was my mother, who encouraged and taught me to read at a very young age and then provided me with several autobiographies as reading materials. These autobiographies expanded the role models from which to choose. This was until I was able to choose my own reading materials. Needless to say, I still find autobiographies fascinating reading and often the source of great inspiration. I should also add, some autobiographies have also showed me qualities that I should not adopt, which incidentally also served as good role models.

WHO IS A ROLE MODEL?

A role model is "a person whose behavior, especially that which is exhibited in a particular capacity, serves as a model or standard for another person to follow." One of the criticisms often made in our society is that there are not many good role models for young people to emulate. In this criticism, the responsibility is placed on adults and on influential people to provide models of behavior that young people want to follow. There may be some merit in this criticism, when older and influential people exhibit behavior that is unbecoming, and sometimes even embarrassing, and that may cause us to ask, "What example is that person showing?"

OUR FAVORITE ROLE MODELS

Most young people have someone they already idolize. It could be because of how that person dresses, sings, acts, or plays a sport. The truth is, celebrities and professional athletes make the most influential role models. While the behavior of some of these role models is admirable, that of others is definitely unacceptable. Despite this, some young people simply adopt attitudes and values they see their favorite sports stars and celebrities displaying. While some role models have positive values, others do not.

DISTINGUISHING BETWEEN ROLE MODELS

A more appropriate approach to having positive role models may be to put greater responsibility on young people for making a conscious effort to choose those that can influence their lives positively. Most young people know the difference between right and wrong. Many who exhibit undesirable behavior know that the behavior is unacceptable and anti-social. But many believe that by displaying this behavior, they are creating an aura that makes them appear 'dangerous' and maybe attractive to their peers. They may try to give the impression that they are above the rules and the law. In some cases, they may be following the behavior that a particular sports star or celebrity readily displays.

HOLDING ONESELF TO A HIGHER STANDARD

But young people must hold themselves to a higher standard and many do. While it is customary to like the way someone sings or to be a fan of a particular basketball player, it is not necessary to accept the morals and way of life of that particular individual. The good that can come from looking at questionable behavior on the part of a star or celebrity that you admire is to see what is wrong with the behavior and avoid it. This does not say that you cannot appreciate that person's talent.

HOW TO CHOOSE POSITIVE ROLE MODELS

The challenge to young people is to see who is influencing the way they behave. On a personal level, you may consider what qualities you find most attractive in this person. You may question whether these qualities are positive or negative, whether you are imitating your star or celebrity in the positive qualities they display. Other questions to consider are: "Are the qualities that you display moving you ahead or holding you back?" "Are these qualities motivating you to excel or are they getting you into trouble?" Be honest with yourself in making this determination.

TIME FOR A CHANGE

As a young person, if the qualities that you are emulating are holding your back, and if these are the qualities that characterize your role model, then you are seriously ready for a change of role model. As Alan C. Page, an associate justice of the Minnesota Supreme Court, the founder of the Page Education Foundation and a member of the NFL Hall of

Fame, once pointed out, "We become whom we emulate; children must be taught that the true heroes are not sports celebrities but people who meet the challenges of real life. . . ." (Page, 1996). There are many sports figures and celebrities that demonstrate admirable qualities that many young people would be proud to emulate. But don't just choose someone as a role model because that person is popular or plays a sport well. Choose as a good role model a person "who meet(s) the challenges of real life." That person does not have to be popular. It could be a parent, a teacher, or anyone who inspires you. As Page (1996) continues, "We should be choosing our role models by the content of their character." This is an advice that young people, and older people, too, should be taking.

CHOOSE WISELY

Choose a role model that will move you ahead. As a leader or a future leader, you must develop positive qualities that would also influence your followers. As Joe DiMaggio, sports figure, observed, "A person always doing his or her best becomes a natural leader, just by example." So plan well, choose wisely, and do the things you know are right, knowing that you can inspire others to become leaders as well.

CHAPTER 1 - FOOD FOR THOUGHT – CHOOSING YOUR ROLE MODEL

TOPICS AND IDEAS FOR SELF-REFLECTION AND DISCUSSION

SELF-REFLECTION

"To change bad habits we must study the habits of successful role models." Jack Canfield

What comes to mind? What would you like to change?

You may be thinking, "I know the bad habits that I have. What do I have to do to change them?" Take your time and figure these out.

"Sometimes our light goes out but is blown into flame by another human being. Each of us owes deepest thanks to those who have rekindled this light." Albert Schweitzer

Think of the people who may have had a positive influence on you or the people whom you admire. What are the qualities that you admire in them and what would you like to change in yourself? Recognize those that have made a positive contribution to the person that you are today and be thankful for this.

15

GROUP DISCUSSION

"Young people need models, not critics." *(John Wooden)*

Think of people whom you may consider as role models.

mom   msn. walker

dr. rob

If you have not yet chosen a role model, think of the qualities that you want to develop and look for the people who most exhibit these qualities. organized

determined

kind

Make a list of these people. Remember, these people do not have to be celebrities. They could be your parents, your friends' parents, your teachers, or just ordinary people you know well.   aunt lyn

mom

uncle joe

Have a group discussion and see what qualities most group members would like to develop. Look at the different individuals that are chosen as role models.

CHAPTER 1 – REFERENCES AND FURTHER READING

Ingram, Jay & Cengemi, Joseph (2012). Emotions, emotional intelligence, and leadership: a brief, pragmatic perspective. *Education, 132*(4), 771-778.

Page, Alan C. (February 23, 1996). Perspective (on heroes). *http://articles. latimes. com/1996-02-23/local/me-38992_1_true-heroes*

Shockness, I. (July 31, 2019). Character is important for youth leadership. Successful Youth Living Blog. Available at*https://www. successfulyouthlivingblog. com/2019/07/31/character-is-important-for-youth-leadership/*

CHAPTER 2

A WINNING ATTITUDE WORKS WONDERS

To be a leader, you need to be able to influence people for good. Having a winning attitude works wonders. We often misunderstand what this means. Usually, when we speak about having a winning attitude, the picture that comes to mind is that of two teams in competition with each other, or two people competing against each other, each wanting to win. There could only be a winner and a loser, and no one wants to be the loser. Therefore, in the case of school teams, many coaches and parents eagerly push their students, children, or young people in their care, to win at all costs.

WHAT IS THE MESSAGE?

"Beat the other team" or "be better than the others" is the message that many young people hear when they are on a team, and over time many of them develop a competitive spirit that makes them want to always win. Many young people are also taught to develop this attitude in their schoolwork, as parents ask if their son or daughter did better than his or her classmates or a specific classmate. Many young people grow up wanting to be better than the other person, to be ahead of the others, and to have more than other people have. These young people often make sore losers, when their teams lose or when they didn't get the best grades, because they value the outcome and not the process. This is not what a winning attitude is all about.

LOSING IS AN IMPORTANT LIFE LESSON

While it is desirable to try to win and not lose, young people have to learn to accept that on occasions they would lose. This is important for life, for no one wins all the time. It is also important for the present as well, since many young people have not learned how to accept losing. Some players who do not know how to lose end up fighting or hurting another player from the winning team. Having a winning attitude often has very little to do with wanting to be better than someone else, or to be on a winning team. A parent asking his or her child whether he or she did better than another child is not instilling a winning attitude. This is merely teaching the child to judge himself or herself in relation to someone else. This could backfire as well, since if a class is not striving, a student may have no motivation to achieve. A winning attitude can be developed by helping a child or young person strive to do better than he or she did the day before, without becoming obsessive about this.

THERE'S NO SUCH THING AS CAN'T

Having a winning attitude has everything to do with how we feel about ourselves, and whether we are willing to try or not. It sometimes has something to do with teams, and with competition, but it always has something to do with what we think of our capabilities. A parent asking his or her child whether the child has improved over the term, or a coach telling his or her players to improve on certain skills, is encouraging the development of a winning attitude.

However, as a young person, you may also be learning that there is no such thing as "can't", that nothing is impossible if you are prepared to put in the effort, and that your goal is to improve. These are thoughts that would help you develop a winning attitude.

MORE TO DISCOVER

Having a winning attitude accomplishes several things. First, it makes you feel that there are many opportunities to be explored and things to discover. You do not have to be intimidated on encountering something new, for you know you could try and find out about it. Rather than saying "I don't know", you can say "I'd find out." *willing to learn*

FEELING CONFIDENT

Next, having a winning attitude makes you feel confident, knowing that it is not out of your control. By putting out the effort, you could influence how you feel. Sometimes, it doesn't happen on the first try. However, on the second or third try it may work. It may take several more attempts, but having a winning attitude means trying something over and over until you get it. *Sounds exhausting*

FEELING GOOD ABOUT YOURSELF

Having a winning attitude makes you feel good about yourself. Not knowing how to do something doesn't mean failure. It means that you haven't yet applied yourself to the task, or that you are in the process of learning.

A WINNING ATTITUDE REALLY WORKS WONDERS

Having a winning attitude works wonders. Here are some ways of thinking that will help develop a winning attitude: "This is something new, and I want to find out how it works, so I'll try it." "This task may be difficult, but if I try, I know I can do it." "Maybe I tried something and it didn't work, but it is something that could be done, so I'll try until I get it."

"I can improve on that shot!" "I played well today, but I know I can do better tomorrow." "I haven't done very well, but I will improve on my next test." All of these thoughts have nothing to do with someone else, and everything to do with you. Having a winning attitude is all about you developing your talents and skills to the best of your abilities.

CHAPTER2 - FOOD FOR THOUGHT – A WINNING ATTITUDE WORKS WONDERS

TOPICS AND IDEAS FOR SELF-REFLECTION AND DISCUSSION

SELF-REFLECTION

"Most of the important things in the world have been accomplished by people who have kept on trying when there seemed no hope at all." Dale Carnegie

"Your attitude determines your altitude." Zig Ziglar

"Attitude is a little thing that makes a big difference." Sir Winston Churchill

(What are some of the important things you have been trying to accomplish and have given up? Maybe it is time to start again?) guitar

bass   knitting

"Anyone who has never made a mistake has never tried anything new." Albert Einstein

You may be thinking, "So, I know I have made many mistakes. I just have to correct these mistakes and move along." Make an effort to do so, but it may not be easy, but well worth it.

GROUP DISCUSSION

Think of people who have been working on projects for a long time and have not given up, and who have been successful in the long run. Make a list of people who have succeeded after great hardships. Discuss within your group.

teeh people

Some group members may decide to form an "Inspiration Group" or "Encouragement Group", where they could encourage each other, especially when they are not succeeding as they would like and may be discouraged.

One of the rules for the group could be that group members always focus on helping each other to perform well and feel good about themselves, even in the face of discouragement.

Another rule could be not to focus on showing how much more they have accomplished than those who may be having a difficult time. Being competitive and boastful could be a source of further discouragement to those who have been striving as hard as they possibly could to succeed and who are not achieving what they believe they should be. Boasting about oneself to another who is having difficulty may not only be discouraging, but could create jealousy.

A third rule could be the understanding among group members that they can feel 'safe' in saying how they really feel in the group setting, knowing that group members would not be judgmental, but truly supportive.

The objective to having this support group within a group is so that people feel that they have somewhere where they could share their struggles and find sympathetic ears and empathic hearts.

CHAPTER 2 – REFERENCES AND FURTHER READING

Harrell, K. (September 22, 2016). Why your attitude is everything. Success. Available at *https://www. success. com/why-your-attitude-is-everything/*

Maxwell, J. C. (1993). The Winning Attitude – Your key to Personal Success. Thomas Nelson Publishers

Simon, G. (July 27, 2015). Winning is a matter of attitude. Counselling Resource. Available at *https://counsellingresource. com/features/2015/07/27/winning-attitude*

CHAPTER 3

DEVELOPING A MINDSET]
SUCCESS

Some people think of success as something that occurs periodically, as when they win a prize or get a coveted award. Although success is often measured in terms of gaining something, it is more than this. It is a way of thinking - a way of life. One can be a success and not always be a winner. A successful person is one who thinks of himself or herself as a success and is always working towards making this a reality. How, then, do we account for the fact that we are not always winning?

WHAT IS SUCCESS?

By defining success, we would find the answer. Success, according to Napoleon Hill and Clement Stone, two motivational speakers, is "the progressive realization of a worthy ideal." It means establishing a goal that one considers important and worthwhile, and working tirelessly towards achieving it. Success is therefore defined personally.

For example, one person may set out to be a highly skilled mechanic, surgeon, or musician, because this is something that he or she has always wanted to be. Another may want to be a good salesperson, an excellent manager, an exceptional parent or an outstanding professional. Regardless of what one sets out to be, to be a success one must be determined to be the best at whatever one does, and continue working to achieve that excellence.

WHY IS GOAL SETTING IMPORTANT?

Why is goal setting so important? Without a specific goal in mind, one would be a wanderer. Hill and Stone provided a very good analogy. Think of a ship setting out with a clear destination. All the crew know exactly what they have to do, when they would leave and when they would arrive. They would keep on schedule and the captain would see to it that the ship leaves and arrives on time. Think of another ship with no destination. In fact, this ship may not even have a captain, or if it does, he or she may not have a fixed plan. It is unlikely that this ship would leave the harbor, or if it does, it would quite likely end up nowhere in particular or even crash on the rocks.

We are like ships, to employ the analogy Hill and Stone used. If we set goals or have specific destinations in mind, we would usually realize our goals or arrive at our predetermined destinations. If we fail to set goals or establish destinations, we would often not accomplish anything. If we have goals, like the ship with a clear destination, we may meet with obstacles.

NO GUARANTEES, BUT A PLAN

One may argue that although we set ourselves a goal, there is no guarantee that we would achieve it. There may be obstacles that could prevent us from moving ahead with our plan. If we use the analogy of the ship, as Hill and Stone used in their work, obstacles should not deter us. When a ship sets sail for a particular destination, if there is an obstacle in its way, the captain does not abandon the ship in mid-ocean. He or she will initiate a change in plan. The ship will take another course, yet the destination would usually be the same. It may take a little longer, but the ship will still arrive.

OBSTACLES NOT A SIGNAL TO STOP

Similarly, when we encounter obstacles in pursuing our goals, we should not take it as a signal to stop. We should simply see it as an indication that we should find another way of accomplishing our goals. Obstacles become opportunities for a change of course, and not as occasions for abandonment of plans.

PERSISTENCE AND COMMITMENT NEEDED

The reason that the ship arrives at its destination is that the captain has persistence and commitment. We would accomplish our goals if we are persistent and committed to achieving them. By setting ourselves worthy goals, and continuously working towards achieving them, we could consider ourselves a success, despite the obstacles that we may face. We develop a mindset for success when we set our personal goals and work to achieve them.

CHAPTER 3 - FOOD FOR THOUGHT – DEVELOPING A MINDSET FOR SUCCESS

TOPICS AND IDEAS FOR SELF-REFLECTION AND DISCUSSION

SELF-REFLECTION

"If you want to be happy, set a goal that commands your thoughts, liberates your energy and inspires your hopes." Andrew Carnegie

Think about what you have accomplished and how much more you can do.

GROUP DISCUSSION

A key achievement could be for group members to engage in their own goal setting, or if they already have goals, to revisit these goals. Group members can review to see if they are achieving these goals, and if not, can identify the obstacles that are blocking their progress, and look for ways of removing these obstacles. This could be an individual or group activity.

CHAPTER 3 – REFERENCES AND FURTHER READING

Briceno, Eduardo – The power of belief – mindset and success. TED Talk x Manhattan Beach – YouTube video – Available at *https://www. youtube. com/watch?v=pN34FNbOKXc*

Cherry, K. (March 2, 2020). Why mindset matters for our success. Available at *https://www. verywellmind. com/what-is-a-mindset-2795025*

Dweck, C. S. (2006). *Mindset: The New Psychology of Success.* New York: Random House Inc.

Hill, N. & Stone, C. (2009). *Success through a Positive Mental Attitude.* New York: Simon & Schuster.

CHAPTER 4

GOAL SETTING

Goal setting is something that younger as well as older people must do, for without a goal, there is no motivation to strive forward. We must look at a goal as a resolution. The dictionary describes 'goal' as 'a thing for which an effort is made,' and a resolution as a 'firmness of purpose,' or as a 'fixed determination.' Looking at a goal in this way, we must see it as something that we are willing to work for with fixed determination. In order to make a resolution work, we have to be very serious about what we are resolving to do or not do. This means establishing a firm goal in our minds, and working towards it. It means establishing steps towards achieving our goal and using certain guidelines to keep us on track.

DECIDE ON A GOAL

The first thing we have to do is to decide on a goal. However, the goal that we may have in mind may be long-term, something that can only be achieved in a matter of years. This is good, but in order to achieve it, we have to break it down into smaller increments or shorter periods.

LONG-TERM GOAL

One of the things we would find very helpful is breaking down our long-term goal into medium-term goals and short-term goals. While long-term goals may be in the range of five years or so, a medium-term goal may be for two years. A short-term goal may be from one to three or even six months. It could also be on a weekly basis. Short-term goals are the small things we do towards accomplishing our medium-term goals, and our medium-term goals are the things we do towards achieving our long-term goal.

An example of how this works is as follows. Suppose you decide that in five years, you should be holding a particular job or having a certain amount of money saved. This is your long-term goal. If you keep this in mind, and have no short-term goals to achieve your long-term goal, you may find at the end of five years you still do not have the job or the money.

MEDIUM-TERM AND LONG-TERM GOALS

Therefore, you must set up a medium-term goal, for example, that at the end of two years, you should be halfway towards reaching this goal. The short-term goal will help you monitor your progress, and will tell you whether you are on track to achieve your medium-term goal. It may indicate to you that you have to do something more if you want to achieve your long-term goal. You could take a similar approach to assessing how well you are on track to realizing your long-term goals. Adjustments are in order to achieve these.

MUST BE SPECIFIC

Whether your goals are long-term, medium-term or short-term, you need to follow certain guidelines. Your goals must be specific, measurable, and realistic. Firstly, your goals must be very specific. It is not sufficient to say, "I want a good job or a lot of money." You must spell it out." I want a job as a computer specialist by December 31, 2025," or "I must have in my possession $100,000 by January 1, 2026."

MUST BE MEASURABLE

Regardless of the goal that you set for yourself, it must be something that you can measure. It is not good enough to say, "I want to be happy," except you have some way of measuring happiness. For example, you may say, I want to complete university or college by June 2023. Therefore, when June 2023 rolls around, you will be able to measure whether you achieved your goal or not.

Whatever goals you set for yourself must be realistic ones. It is no use saying to yourself that you want to be president or prime minister of your country by 2025, if you are just entering high school this year. No amount of wishing will make this happen. However, if you tell yourself that in two years you would have completed a certificate program that you are presently enrolled in, or that you would be promoted to Grade 12 with an improved report card next school year, with specific grades assigned to your subjects, then this is a realistic goal you would strive towards achieving. Or you may tell yourself that in January 2025, you will have your own catering or computer business. This is realistic if you have the requisite skills or if you intend to put in the effort to get the necessary skills.

PLANNING TO ACHIEVE SPECIFIC, MEASURABLE, AND REALISTIC GOALS

Once you have established your goal, you have to plan how to achieve it. If it is a certain kind of job, then you must plan to undertake the proper course of study that would prepare you to hold that job. If you already have the knowledge, then you would set about getting a job, and developing the strategy for putting your plan into action. Regardless of your plan, you have to take action.

CHAPTER 4 - FOOD FOR THOUGHT – GOAL SETTING

TOPICS AND IDEAS FOR SELF-REFLECTION AND DISCUSSION

SELF-REFLECTION

Make a specific plan for your goals.

"Our goals can only be reached through a vehicle of a plan in which we must fervently believe, and upon which we must vigorously act. There is no other route to success." Pablo Picasso

"A goal without a plan is just a wish." Antoine de Saint-Exupéry

(I MUST TAKE ACTION NOW!)

GROUP DISCUSSION

Take goal setting to a much deeper level. Think of the goals you have set. Then go back and review what goals you want to accomplish on a short term, medium term and long term basis. Really think carefully on how you would measure successful attainment of those goals. Print out a copy of your plan and stick it on a mirror or in a place where you would see it often.

CHAPTER 4 – REFERENCES AND FURTHER READING

Nowack, K. (2017). Facilitating successful behavior change: Beyond goal setting to goal flourishing. *Consulting Psychology Journal: Practice and Research, 69*(3), 153-171. *https://www. apa. org/pubs/highlights/spotlight/issue-101*

Rader, L. A. (2005). Goal setting for students and teachers: Six steps to success. *The Clearing House, 78*(3), 123-126.

Riopel, L. (January 9, 2020). The importance, benefits, and value of goal setting. Positive Psychology. Available at *https://positivepsychology. com/benefits-goal-setting/*

CHAPTER 5

PERSISTENCE, A DESIRABLE TRAIT

At a Board of Trade black-tie dinner hosted in his honor several years ago, Ted Rogers, then head of Rogers Communications, as Man of the Year, reportedly revealed some of the factors that were responsible for making him a multimillionaire and a success in business. One of the factors that he stressed was that of persistence, which he explained was a desirable quality to have. Persistence, while indispensable in the corporate world, is just as pertinent in the academic world and elsewhere. Students of all ages would benefit from cultivating this quality.

HABIT OF MIND

Persistence is really a habit of mind, which is based on the individual adopting a singleness of purpose and direction, and continuing to put out effort in whatever project or task he or she is undertaking, regardless of the difficulty. Persistence is an easy quality to exhibit, when one is experiencing success, since success in itself motivates one to stay with whatever one is doing. The true test of persistence is to stay with something even when things are not going well, or when things seem to be going wrong. There are many instances when things go wrong, and when one's first instinct is to give up.

COPING WITH YOUR CHALLENGES

As a younger student, you may be having a very difficult time understanding integers. You may be a high school student who is having a rough time of it getting over calculus in your final year. Or maybe you are at university and are having a difficult time understanding statistics. Or you may be a nursing student who is finding your clinical placement a real challenge.

DON'T GIVE UP

Don't give up!! Stick with the subject or the course of work you have undertaken. Accept the challenge and if you stay with it long enough and remain focused enough, you will find that you will finally understand it. One day things would fall into place, and it would appear as though a light has gone on. Then, you may wonder how it was that it took you so long for you to understand it.

DECLARE IT AND ACCOMPLISH IT

Persistence means convincing yourself that regardless of how difficult a task appears to be, that it is not impossible, and that you will do it. Once you declare that you would accomplish something, it appears that determination becomes etched on your mind, and it helps you muster sufficient effort to accomplish your task.

RESONATES WITH ALL

Although when Mr. Rogers spoke about the importance of persistence, he was speaking to a group of business people, his message is relevant and resonates with students and people in all walks of life even today. Many students change courses when they encounter difficulty, choosing instead courses that are easier. Some students give up school altogether, believing that they do not have what it takes to make a success in the academic field. In these cases, some individuals give up just before they encounter a real breakthrough and miss out on the benefits of their earlier efforts. We should all take comfort in the expression that "the darkest watch of the night is just before the dawn."

EVIDENCE OF PERSISTENCE IN THE CLASSROOM

In order to be successful in analyzing and solving the problem, the individual must possess 16 habits of mind, with persistence being one of the most important. In order to promote persistence and the other habits of mind, there are five skills that are necessary, namely, value, inclination, sensitivity, capability and commitment (Mohl, 2009). A student displays persistence by sticking with the problem that appears difficult and resisting the temptation to lament, "I don't get it!" or to quickly ask the teacher, "What do we do next?" or simply express dismay that "I don't know we were supposed to do this." These expressions can be seen as evidence of not using persistence to seek out answers to a problem that may appear difficult at the outset.

The student who uses persistence is inclined to continue trying to find the answer on his or her own, to demonstrate capability to work through the problem and to be committed to finding the solution at the end. This goes for students as well as for other individuals who encounter problems in life.

PERSISTENCE CAN MAKE THE DIFFERENCE

Therefore, whether you are a student in high school, college or university, or a new graduate entering a new profession, or someone dealing with a family problem or challenge, remember that persistence is a very valuable habit of mind that could see you through many difficult times. It could make the difference between failure and success in whatever you undertake.

As Calvin Coolidge, 30th US President, summed it up nicely:

"Nothing in the world can take the place of persistence. Talent will not; nothing is more common than unsuccessful men with talent. Genius will not; unrewarded genius is almost proverb. Education will not; the world is full of educated derelicts. Persistence and determination alone are omnipotent." Therefore, be persistent in all that you do.

CHAPTER 5 - FOOD FOR THOUGHT – PERSISTENCE, A DESIRABLE TRAIT

TOPICS AND IDEAS FOR SELF-REFLECTION AND DISCUSSION

SELF-REFLECTION

"Patience, persistence, and perspiration make an unbeatable combination for success." Napoleon Hill

"Victory belongs to the most persevering." Napoleon Bonaparte

"Making your mark on the world is hard. If it were easy, everybody would do it. But it's not. It takes patience, it takes commitment, and it comes with plenty of failure along the way. The real test is not whether you avoid this failure, because you won't. It's whether you let it harden or shame you into inaction, or whether you learn from it; whether you choose to persevere." Barack Obama

You may say to yourself, "I know I have talent, but if I don't stick with my dreams, I may still lose out. Time for a change."

GROUP DISCUSSION

Using 'GROUP' to illustrate 'PERSISTENCE'. The various words on the left illustrate "Persistence", but with slightly different nuances. Complete the sentence beside each word to show your commitment to demonstrating persistence. Share with your group or you can do this on your own.

Grit, Resolved, Ongoing, Unfluctuating, Patience, Strong-willed – are all related to persistence.

G – Grit – I will display grit in

....

R – Resolved – I am resolved to undertake

....

O – Ongoing – I will be ongoing in my effort to

....

U – Unfluctuating – I will be unfluctuating in

....

P – Patience – I will demonstrate patience in

....

S – Strong-willed – I will be strong-willed when.

....

CHAPTER 5 – REFERENCES AND FURTHER READING

Mohl, M. (September 2009). Getting into the habit of persistence. *Science Scope, 33(1): Critical Thinking.* National Science Teachers Association.

Roland, N. , Frenay, M. & Boudrenghien, G. (2016). Toward a better understanding of academic persistence among Fresh-man: A qualitative approach. *Journal of Education and Training Studies, 4*(12).

Wayt, L. (2012). The impact of students' academic and social relationships on college student persistence. Available at *https://digitalcommons. unl. edu/cgi/viewcontent. cgi?article=1108&context=cehsedaddiss*

CHAPTER 6

THE VALUE OF BEING THOROUGH

"Being thorough" is a habit that can permeate everything we do, and can pay huge dividends in every stage of our lives. Students can develop this habit, but they sometimes need encouragement. How can "being thorough" pay off for students? As educators would agree, the students who do best at school are the ones that go about their work conscientiously, the ones that make sure they do all that is required of them, and more.

ACCURACY AND PRECISION

Being thorough is really a habit of mind that contributes to excellence or success in undertakings and can be described as "striving for accuracy and precision". This striving for accuracy and precision, this desire to be thorough, is a characteristic that exemplifies those who take pride in what they are doing, and whose craftsmanship displays commitment to excellence. This is an important characteristic for young people, particularly in their classes and courses.

FAILING BECAUSE NOT THOROUGH

In many years of working with young people, I still come across students who are failing miserably simply because they are not thorough in what they do. They attempt the work that is assigned, but do not take the time to complete everything that is asked. In many cases, these students do the minimum, simply to say that they did the work, but do not take pride in having completed everything. This could have serious implications.

Take, for example, working with a short story or novel. Some students may read through a story, understand it completely, including being able to answer the higher level questions. However, when they are asked a question, they give the briefest of responses. Very often, these responses are so brief that the teacher cannot determine whether the student really understood the story or is just hazarding a guess. In many instances, if the student takes the time to make the connection in writing between what he or she understands and what is being asked, the student would be able to prove that he or she has a good understanding of the story.

TEACHERS NOT MIND READERS

Teachers are not expected to be mind readers, and so should not be expected to make the connection for the student. If a student is not making the connection in answering the question, then the teacher could only assume that the student doesn't know and maybe didn't even take the time to read the story. Yet, in many cases, if the teacher or someone else were to ask the student the same question, the student would be able to verbalize the answer fully and correctly.

PARTIAL ANSWERS DON'T WORK

Answering a question only partially is another example of not being thorough. A student may be asked a question that consists of two parts, or that may involve the discussion of several concepts. If the student reads only part of the question or deals with only one of the concepts, the student would very likely not perform well. The student would have failed to be thorough in addressing the whole assignment.

SHORTCUTS ARE DECEIVING

Or a student may decide to look at the questions before doing the assigned reading and may even try to answer the questions without thoroughly reading through the text. Or the student may rifle through the reading and try to locate the answers without gaining a full understanding of the concepts or of what action is taking place in the reading. The student may then merely copy words or sentences out of the reading and supply them as an answer to a question containing similar words and sentences. With emphasis on plagiarism these days, a student may simply try changing the words. However, these gimmicks cannot be substitutes for being thorough.

ERROR IN ANSWER IS NO EXCUSE

In math, a student may understand a concept and may work out a problem involving that concept. However, in putting down the answer, he or she may make a simple error in a basic operation. The student may get the problem wrong and may be quite upset because he or she knew how to do the problem. "I only made a small mistake writing down the answer and the teacher gave me zero on the question!" A more lenient teacher may assign half the points for the question. Had the student been thorough, he or she would have looked over the answer to make sure that the work was done correctly. It is very likely that the student would have recognized the error and would have corrected it.

"BETTER LATE THAN NEVER"

Being thorough is a habit that could be formed early in life, but the proverb, "Better late than never" can apply here. As a student who is normally not thorough, you can make a change now. You can decide to start being thorough by not looking for shortcuts and not doing sloppy work. It will mean taking pride in whatever you do, making sure you do everything well. Being thorough is a habit that can pay huge dividends in adolescence as well as in adulthood. Therefore, as a young person, developing a habit that will serve you well as you grow older makes good sense.

CHAPTER 6 - FOOD FOR THOUGHT – THE VALUE OF BEING THOROUGH

Topics and Ideas for Self-Reflection and Discussion

SELF-REFLECTION

"There is no shortcut to achievement. Life requires thorough preparation – veneer isn't worth anything?" George Washington Carver

GROUP DISCUSSION

"Whatever work you undertake, do it seriously, thoroughly and well; never leave it half-done or undone, never feel yourself satisfied unless and until you have given it your very best. Cultivate the habits of discipline and toleration. Surrender not the convictions you hold dear but learn to appreciate the points of view of your opponents. "Syama Prasad Mukherjee

Discuss this quote with your group. How do people feel about it, and what situations do they believe to be appropriate for taking this approach.

CHAPTER 6 – REFERENCES AND FURTHER READING

Alhamlan, S. , Aljasser, H. , Almajed, A. , Almansour, H. & Alahmad, N. (2018). A Systematic Review: Using Habits of Mind to Improve Student's thinking in Class. *Higher Education Studies, 8*(1), 25-35.

Costa, A. L. (2021). What are Habits of Mind? The Institute for Habits of Mind. Available at *https://www. habitsofmindinstitute. org/about-us/hear-art/*

Fletcher, J. (2013). Critical Habits of Mind: Exposing the Process of Development. *Liberal Education, 99*(1), 1-5. Association of American Colleges & Universities: A Voice and a force for Liberal Education.

Heick, T. (October 19, 2012). Integrating the 16 Habits of Mind: A quick tour of Costa and Kallick's 16 Habits of Mind, along with suggestions for implementing them as classroom best practices. Edutopia. Available at *https://www. edutopia. org/blog/habits-of-mind-terrell-heick*

CHAPTER 7

CONFORMITY BREEDS MEDIOCRITY

Dare to be different! Generally, we are taught to conform: everyone doing the same thing the same way. In fact, conformity is often viewed as a sign of being properly socialized, because we accept what society is doing as the norm, and conform by displaying the same behavior as others. Unfortunately, not everything that society does is the best that can be done.

NOT JUST GETTING BY

One of the problems is that we promote the value of getting by with doing as little as we possibly can. When some people boast about having a good job, one of the characteristics they often mention is having very little to do. To people who look forward to a job that is fulfilling, having little to do can be really boring. Employees who may want to work hard are sometimes cautioned by their co-workers not to 'rock the boat', and not to show them up.

NOT MUCH TO DO?

Similarly, some students see a good day at school as one where they didn't have much to do. Also, having no homework is seen as a good thing. Most students prefer being asked to do only a few short questions rather than a longer assignment. Students who want to work, who want to learn as much as possible, and who put out the effort, are often branded as "nerds", "brainers", and the like. They are often not popular. On the other hand, in many instances, the students that are often the most popular are not always the students who aspire to be exceptional academically. However, if the values of a school or other institution include academic excellence, then students who aspire to this excellence are not teased but respected.

WE ARE ALL UNIQUE

We are all unique because of our particular experiences, our families, and our ideas. It follows that we would be different in the values that we have and the goals to which we aspire. Yet, so dominating are the values in our society that from an early age we may discard the values that our parents may have tried to instill in us. Many parents encourage their children on a daily basis to aspire to greater things, and to be more than mediocre. Some children take heed, while others simply turn a deaf ear. However, while some parents encourage their children to excel and aspire to greater things, these very parents take the route of mediocrity in their jobs, something of which their children are well aware.

FOLLOWING THE CROWD OFTEN DOESN'T LEAD VERY FAR

Following the crowd may seem as the right thing to do, but it often doesn't lead very far. People who seek jobs that are not challenging and that offer very little to do should not complain when their jobs disappear. Young people who are content to get away with doing as little as possible in class would find out that they know far less than they should know.

BE A LEADER

Don't be afraid to be the leader, to be different, and to aspire to excellence when everyone around you is trying to just get by. Whether you are a student, an employee, a young person, whoever you are, try to excel at whatever you do. You can do more than just get by. Think of the things you can improve. Think of ways you can improve yourself. You don't have to be stuck in a dead-end job, when you can create your own prospects! As a student, you don't have to be barely passing! You can excel. In short, you don't have to be content with barely making it, because others are! You can strive to be the best that you can be. If you are in a work situation as a leader, you may think of ways that you can motivate your team to handle mediocrity. You may find that one of the best ways of doing this is to also encourage team members to be the best that they can be. You may find that the same qualities that make you avoid mediocrity and seek excellence are the same qualities that help your team members to excel as well. Put in the extra effort that will make the difference, and dare to be different!

CHAPTER 7 - FOOD FOR THOUGHT – CONFORMITY BREEDS MEDIOCRITY

TOPICS AND IDEAS FOR SELF-REFLECTION AND DISCUSSION

SELF-REFLECTION

"People who are unable to motivate themselves must be content with mediocrity, no matter how impressive their other talents." Andre Carnegie

"The quality of a person's life is in direct proportion to their commitment to excellence, regardless of their chosen field of endeavor."

Vince Lombardi

"Without enthusiasm, you are doomed to a life of mediocrity, but with it you can accomplish miracles." Og Mandino

"Don't bother just to be better than your contemporaries or predecessors. Try to be better than yourself." William Faulkner

GROUP DISCUSSION

"Nothing can stop the man with the right mental attitude from achieving his goal; nothing on earth can help the man with the wrong mental attitude."
Thomas Jefferson

What are some of the ways you motivate yourselves?

Have members of the group brainstorm and then open the floor for discussion.

Possible Motivational books to Read: Normal Vincent Peale, The Power of Positive Thinking

Napoleon Hill, Think and Grow Rich.

Earl Nightingale, The Strangest Secret.

Napoleon Hill and Clement Stone, Success through a Positive Mental Attitude.

There are numerous books on positive thinking; some are new and some older.

See how many ways people motivate themselves. You may find some interesting ones that you may be able to use.

CHAPTER 7 – REFERENCES AND FURTHER READING

Munim, W. (March 13, 2018). Say No to Mediocrity and Yes to Excellence. LinkedIn. Available at *https://www. linkedin. com/pulse/say-mediocrity-yes-excellence-waqi-munim*

Lambourne, W. (July 16, 2018). Four steps in handling mediocrity on your team. Legitimate Leadership. Available at *https://www. legitimateleadership. com/2018/07/16/four-steps-in-handling-mediocrity-on-your-team*

Novaes, D. (September 3, 2014). Five tips that will free you from mediocrity. Young Entrepreneur Council. Available at *https://www. forbes. com/sites/theyec/2014/09/03/five-tips-that-will-free-you-from-mediocrity/?sh=5572baae465a*

CHAPTER 8

FORGET LIMITATIONS

~ YOUNG WOMEN ~

Many young women today do not undertake certain tasks, do not enter certain professions, or carry out certain roles, because they are afraid of not being accepted, or may be afraid of not measuring up to expectations. Some believe that these tasks, professions and roles are part of a man's world, and that it takes a man to be successful in these areas. Even if they know they can do it, many women are reluctant to aspire, for fear of being rejected.

But things have been changing, as many young women have been moving into professions and positions that they were not able to attain in the past. Yet, there is still room for improvement, for as noted, the changes that were once dramatic are slowing (Bailey & DiPrete, 2016). Although some women are achieving remarkable positions, a large part of this population is still behind.

HIDE THEIR KNOWLEDGE

Many girls and young women hide their knowledge or fail to make it known. Some girls in high school are under the impression that to appear attractive, they also have to appear to be not very bright, for fear of not attracting certain boyfriends. On the other hand, there are other girls who are forging ahead, and who are discarding, or are not even considering, limitations. These girls want to reach their potential and they are not afraid of appearing to be bright students who excel.

BRILLIANT GIRLS PRETENDING NOT TO KNOW

I have seen this firsthand, where brilliant 15-year old girls in a co-ed class pretended not to know the work, when I knew these girls were knowledgeable on the subject being discussed. Later confessions revealed the girls did not want to appear to be too bright, considering that they felt the boys in the class were very likely less knowledgeable. They feared making the boys feel inadequate and spoiling their chances of getting boyfriends.

CONGRATULATIONS TO GIRLS AND WOMEN WHO ASPIRE TO EXCEL

"Congratulations" to the girls and young women who aspire to reach their potential, who choose career paths that are considered non-traditional for women, and who are claiming their rightful places in society." Congratulations" must also go to the girls and young women who follow traditional occupations and who are making changes to improve the way these occupations and professions are viewed.

CONGRATULATIONS TO BOYS AND MEN WHO GIVE SUPPORT

While there is still systemic discrimination against women, there are many boys and men who are making efforts to eradicate these antiquated ideas and practices, and who accept and make girls and women feel welcomed in different situations and professions. Those men in traditionally male-dominated professions who embrace equity and hire women to fill top level positions must be recognized for making important changes. Males who enter traditionally female-dominated professions also have an impact on changing perceptions of these professions, particularly when they fill non-top-level positions.

MANY WOMEN ARE STILL NOT GIVEN A CHANCE

Many younger and even older women sometimes find that they are limited in the positions that they can hold. Even when they are educated and well qualified to hold important and leadership positions, they find that they are only hired for lower level and temporary positions. Part of the reason for this is the old perception that women are only able to carry out certain roles.

SOME WOMEN STILL ACCEPT LIMITATIONS

Still yet, there are far too many young women who are placing limitations on what they can do. Many are selling themselves short and continue to hold on to old ideas. They limit their aspirations. This, in turn, limits what they can achieve. Many of these women eventually pass on to their sons and daughters ideas that perpetuate the myth of inequalities in gender abilities. Consequently, the vicious cycle of gender myths continues for yet another generation! On the other hand, there are many mothers, some of whom may not have achieved their goals, but who are helping their daughters to reach their potential.

OLD MESSAGES STILL RING LOUDLY

Some young women may have been told as children that they wouldn't achieve much in life. Even though the message may not have been verbal, many women recognized it all the same. Expectations of the traditional roles that women should play in society may have limited their aspirations. There is nothing wrong with women choosing a strictly traditional kind of life. It is a personal choice, but they should know that there are alternatives available to them. Examples of women who have made great achievements in their lives stand out as evidence that women can take advantages of opportunities and could make their own opportunities.

SOME WOMEN CAN REALIZE AND ARE REALIZING THEIR DREAMS

Some women know in their hearts that they have much to offer in other areas of life and that they can pursue a career and make a major contribution to their family, community and country. Many are carrying out both traditional and new roles and are doing so comfortably. Some women experience conflict having a family and a career, while others do so as best they can. Others have left their professions in order to raise their families. Others are able to function well because of the assistance they receive from their spouses. Other women are doing it on their own. Regardless of their situations and their life choices, young women must be aware of the many possibilities that are available to them from the examples they see in other women's lives. Many women are realizing their dreams with or without support.

WHAT'S HOLDING YOU BACK?

If you are a young woman thinking about your future, and not making much headway, ask yourself, "what is holding me back?" You may not like the answer you get. But the answer could be that you need to do something about it. Break out of your limitations and negativity, if this is your situation. As Napoleon Hill and Clement Stone pointed out, "What the human mind can conceive, the human mind can achieve". If you can conceive of yourself doing something, then it is a goal you can achieve.

Go for it! What you need is the determination to make it work. Look at the examples of women who have made it or who are making it at present. Use them as your mentors.

WOMEN WHO ARE REALIZING THEIR DREAMS

There are women who have achieved leadership positions in many walks of life. Many have started at the bottom and have worked hard to achieve their dreams, despite great odds. Some women have applied themselves fully to their goals and have achieved them. In 2020, Kamala Harris, a woman of Black and Asian heritage, has been elected Vice President of the United States, the first woman to hold this high office. This important accomplishment can be a catalyst for young girls and women to see themselves as having a chance to achieve their dreams, regardless of these dreams.

The Young Professionals Committee of the Council on Tall Buildings and Human Habitat developed a lecture series in New York to "showcase some of the exemplary work done by women in the tall building field" (Can-Standard & Dolejsova (2017). In their presentation, these authors show how many of the women identified the obstacles and setbacks they may have faced in this male-dominated field, but highlight some young professional women who stand out.

For example, there are Pascale Sablan, an architect in New York City, who "follow(ed) in the empowered lineage of architect Norma Sklarek (the first licensed female African-American architect in 1954)"; Nicole Dosso, architect at Skidmore, Owings and Merrill in New York; and architect Sara Beardsley of Adrian Smith + Gordon Gill Architecture in

Chicago – all of whom have achieved great accomplishments in the tall building field and in urbanism (Can-Standard & Dolejsova, 2017). These are female architects that are working in the traditional male-dominated field of tall buildings and are excelling.

CAREER OPTIONS FOR WOMEN

Today, women have many career options that were once closed to them, that were not publicized, or that are new. Some of these career options include aviation, biotechnology, engineering, robotics and automation, railway, marine transportation, steel, heavy equipment, and mining (Described and Captioned Media Program, 2021). Seeking out mentors in many of these sectors could also help young women make unique career choices.

Women already in these and other fields can be leaders that will help other young women make right decisions to aspire to their goals, whatever these goals may be.

CHAPTER 8 - FOOD FOR THOUGHT – FORGET LIMITATIONS ~ YOUNG WOMEN ~

TOPICS AND IDEAS FOR SELF-REFLECTION AND DISCUSSION

SELF-REFLECTION

"It took me quite a long time to develop a voice, and now that I have it, I am not going to be silent." — Madeleine Albright

"I've come to believe that each of us has a personal calling that's as unique as a fingerprint – and that the best way to succeed is to discover what you love and then find a way to offer it to others in the form of service, working hard, and also allowing the energy of the universe to lead you." Oprah Winfrey

". . . it's good to have female or minority role models. But the important thing is to have mentors who care about you, and they come in all colors." Condoleezza Rice

GROUP DISCUSSION

Discuss the changes that have taken place and that have led to women moving ahead in the world.

Make a list of women who have excelled. Choose to do a biography on one of these women. Each group member should find a different woman to write about. These should then be shared in different meetings of the group.

CHAPTER 8 – REFERENCES AND FURTHER READING

Bailey, M. J. & DiPrete, T. A. (2016). Five decades of remarkable but slowing change in U. S. Women's economic and social status and political participation. *RSF: The Russell Sage Foundation Journal of the Social Sciences, 2*(4): A half century of change in the lives of American women, 1-32.

Bevan, V. & Learmonth, M. (2013). 'I wouldn't say it's sexism, except that … It's all these little subtle things: Health are scientists' accounts of gender in healthcare science laboratories. *Social Studies of Science, 43*(1), 136-158.

Can-Standard, I. & Dolejsova, M. (2017). ASPECT: RATIOS – Voices of women in the Tall Building World. Council on Tall Buildings & Human Habitat: *CTBUH Journal, 3: Special Issue: Women in the Tall Building Industry,* 44-51.

Described and Captioned Media Program (2021). Career Options for women: emerging Opportunities. Available at *https://dcmp. org/series/198-career-options-for-women-emerging-opportunities*

Fox, R. L. & Lawless, J. L. (2014). Uncovering the origins of the gender gap in political ambition. *The American Political Science Review, 108*(3), 499-519.

Joshi, A. (2014). By whom and when is women;' expertise recognized? The interactive effects of gender and education in Science and engineering teams. *Administrative Science Quarterly, 59*(2), 202-239.

Parekh, S. (Fall 2011). Getting to the Root of Gender Inequality: Structural Injustice and Political Responsibility in Global Justice. *Hypatia, 26*(4), 672-689.

CHAPTER 9

INTEGRITY CANNOT BE BOUGHT

As a society, we think of things of value, things of worth, as things that have a big price tag. In fact, we have become so materialistic that we discard as unimportant things that cannot be bought or sold. Yet, if we think very carefully, we would realize that it is the things of greatest value that cannot be bought or sold. Love and friendship are two of the most obvious. Integrity is just as important.

WHAT IS INTEGRITY?

The dictionary describes integrity as 'sincerity', 'uprightness', 'freedom of deceit or fraud', and 'straightforwardness'. In other words, a person of integrity is a straightforward person, who does not try to deceive another or behave in a fraudulent manner. A person of integrity says what he or she means, does not engage in double-talk, and does not try to be vague in order to cause confusion in the minds of others for his or her gain. A person of integrity is a person who keeps his or her word, who stands by what he or she says and believes. A person of integrity is also a person who can be trusted. Even in situations where a person could take advantage of another, probably because of the other person's naiveté, a person of integrity would refrain from cashing in on the other person's ignorance.

BEING IN THE RIGHT IS NOT EVERYTHING

In our capitalist society, where the saying 'dog eat dog' seems to describe our behavior, many people seem caught up in the race to 'get' the other person, before the other person 'gets' him or her. Being in the right or having the law on one's side is important. However, there are times when people take action against others, deprive others of their goods and property, and use technicalities in law to justify their actions. Recognizing the ignorance or confusion on the part of others, many institutions and individuals swap their integrity for dollars. They literally steal from others, using loopholes to take advantage and defraud unsuspecting others.

COMPROMISING INTEGRITY

We sometimes compromise our integrity even on small matters. We may have bought something, and recognized that the sales clerk had made an error. Rather than give back the money, we count it as gain for ourselves, quieting our consciences by arguing that taking back the money would only get the sales clerk fired. Or we may have found a wallet or a purse with money and other documents in it, and whereas we may have returned it if it had only $40, we may have decided to keep it because it had $400. We saw it as a prize. In this case, we would have swapped our integrity for $400.

SACRIFICING A FRIENDSHIP

Or we may have made an oral agreement to repay a loan to a friend, but after receiving the loan, we begrudged paying it back. Since our friend may not have insisted on a promissory note, and may not have proof of having made the loan, we saw this as an opportunity not to repay. After all, our friend may have no basis for taking us to court. When we behaved this way, we sacrificed a friendship and our integrity for a few dollars. Surely friendship and integrity are worth much more than money could buy!

BE A LEADER: QUESTION YOURSELF

Our integrity is being challenged every day, sometimes more so than at other times, and every day we have to make decisions. If we think of ourselves as persons of integrity, we must think very seriously about our actions. Are we being sincere and upright in what we say and do? Are we free from deceit? Are we being straightforward? Are we behaving in a manner that we can be proud of? Can we honestly look ourselves in the mirror and say, "I am a person of integrity, a person that can be trusted!"?

COSTS NOTHING, BUT WORTH MORE THAN MONEY CAN BUY

Integrity, like love and friendship, is something that costs nothing, but it is worth more than money could buy. Integrity is not dependent on how much money we have. Fortunately, this puts integrity within the reach of everyone, whether rich or poor. Let us treat integrity as something valuable that we cannot afford to lose. It is worth everything we have, and more!

MAKE INTEGRITY A MAJOR BUILDING BLOCK

Therefore, as a young person, embarking on your adult life, use integrity as a major building block, and you won't regret it. You will be known, and you will know yourself, as a person who can be trusted, and whose word means something. As Dwight D. Eisenhower, former U. S. president observed: "The supreme quality for leadership is unquestionably integrity. Without it, no real success is possible, whether it is on a section gang, a football field, in an army, or in an office."

CHAPTER 9 - FOOD FOR THOUGHT – INTEGRITY CANNOT BE BOUGHT

TOPICS AND IDEAS FOR SELF-REFLECTION AND DISCUSSION

SELF-REFLECTION

"I believe that unarmed truth and unconditional love will have the final word in reality. That is why right, temporarily defeated, is stronger than evil triumphant." Martin Luther King, Jr.

"As I have said, the first thing is to be honest with yourself. You can never have an impact on society if you have not changed yourself. Great peacemakers are all people of integrity, of honesty, but humility." Nelson Mandela

You may ask yourself, "Am I a person of integrity? What things do I do that make me think of myself as having integrity. If I am not a person of integrity now, what can I do to become a person of integrity? Or is it too late for me?"

GROUP DISCUSSION

Discuss in a group setting what integrity is. Give examples of integrity and discuss how you can show yourself as a person of integrity.

What are some of the things a person can do to change their reputation and become a person of integrity?

CHAPTER 9 – REFERENCES AND FURTHER READING

Christie, K. (n. d.). Leading with Integrity. Centre for Social Impact – Integrity – Innovation – Investment. Queen's School of Business. Available at *https://smith. queensu. ca/insight/file/qsbinsight whitepaper leading with integrity. pdf*

Folkman, Z. (2021). Honesty and integrity build a foundation of trust. The Clemmer Group. Available at *https://www. clemmergroup. com/articles/honesty-integrity-build-foundation-trust/*

Huberts, L. W. J. C. (2018). Integrity: What it is and Why it is important. Public Integrity, 20 (Issue Sup 1: International Colloquium on ethical leadership: Past, Present and future of Ethics Research). Available at*https://doi. org/10. 1080/10999922. 2018. 1477404*

CHAPTER 10

USING YOUR MINDS

One of the most important tasks we carry out each day is that of thinking. It is thinking that sets us apart from other primates. It is also thinking that allows us to make decisions every minute of the day. Since it takes place automatically, we often take it for granted. Yet, it is such an important process and has such significant consequences that we ought to give it greater consideration.

UNLOCKING THE POWER OF OUR MINDS

If we could improve our thinking, we would find that our decisions are better, and that we become more effective in what we say and do. In other words, if we understand more about our thinking process, we could unlock the power of our minds. Here are some thinking tools that could help us achieve just this. Some refer to these tools as habits of mind; others see these as thinking tools or as strategies for critical thinking.

REFLECTION

The first tool is reflection. We must reflect on our process of thinking. When we are faced with a problem or a new situation, do we panic and find it difficult to think clearly, or do we start analyzing the different parts of the problem or the new situation? Do we approach it methodically, making sure that we look at all aspects of the problem or situation? By reflecting on how we think, we could make changes to think more clearly when faced with problems or new situations.

PERSISTENCE

Another effective thinking tool is that of persistence. When we have a problem or new situation, do we become frustrated and give up? If we do, then we do not find the solution and do not understand the situation. We must recognize that there will often be trial and error, and that we must be prepared to undertake the thinking that supports this. Being persistent means sticking with the problem or new situation until we understand it.

An example of this may be seen in the case of the young person who is learning to do equations, and who is ready to give up because he or she does not know how to solve for x. Or it may be the case of a young man learning to play football, and deciding to give up because he has difficulty passing the ball or learning the plays. Persistence in thinking involves being able to stay with a problem or new situation and trying to work it out or improve the situation.

CONTROLLING IMPULSIVITY

Thinking tool number three is "Controlling impulsivity!" Managing our impulsivity is another thinking tool that helps in many ways. Simply put, this thinking tool requires that we take time to think before we act or respond. It means taking time to consider a problem or a new situation, to understand it, and on the basis of studying it, to make sounder decisions.

A teacher may discourage impulsivity by requiring that students not push their hands up right after a question is asked, but by requiring them to wait for a minute or so before answering. The reasoning is that the student would think about the question in order to formulate an answer. This would often require that the student think more critically about the question. Managing impulsivity involves thinking more thoroughly about the problem or situation instead of making a rash decision.

LISTENING

Listening is another thinking tool, because it allows the individual to be understanding and sensitive to what is being said. Listening should be distinguished from hearing, for while we may hear something, we may not be paying attention to what is actually being said and may not understand its significance or implications. An individual who thinks about what is being said is well on his or her way to developing his or her thinking process, because this individual would be asking questions.

QUESTIONING

Questioning is yet another important thinking tool because it takes us beyond accepting what we are told. It involves our asking the questions 'what', 'how', 'why' and 'what if', and getting answers that would probably lead us to ask even more questions. For young people, this is particularly interesting, because it is this questioning that promotes curiosity or wonderment about the world. Curiosity leads to further investigation and to the development of creativity. Creativity unleashes the imagination and causes the individual to be inventive. This process is the very foundation for learning.

BEING ACCURATE

Being accurate is another thinking tool. Persistence, managing impulsivity, listening, questioning, being curious and creative are all thinking tools that are enhanced when we check for accuracy. By going over what we have thought about or have done, we have the opportunity to see where there may have been errors in judgment, or possible confusion. We also have the opportunity to see where there may have been possible innovations and creative solutions.

KEEPING AN OPEN MIND

Keeping an open mind is yet another thinking tool because it makes us flexible and receptive to new ideas. This is an important consideration, whether we are young people or adults, students or professionals, employees or employers. Knowledge is continually being increased, and if we believe we know it all, then we are doomed to ignorance. Having an open mind keeps us always thinking and learning, and makes us aware of innovations. It also lays the foundation for our creation of knowledge through our thinking.

DRAWING ON PAST KNOWLEDGE

Another thinking tool is that of drawing on past knowledge. This includes past experience. When we are faced with a problem or a new situation, we must use what we already know. Past experience serves us well here, for if we had made mistakes or experienced failures in the past, we would know what to avoid. This provides us with a good foundation on which to build, and so we could proceed to use the other thinking tools to make sound decisions.

EXPERIENCE THE WORLD FULLY

Increasing the power of our minds goes further than this. It involves our being able to experience the world fully. Thinking is not one-dimensional, but rather involves input from all our senses. We should therefore engage our sight, our hearing, and our senses of touch, smell and taste when we think.

COMMUNICATION

Another tool is communicating our thoughts. This tool is important to the thinking process, for in order to communicate our ideas clearly to others, we would have had to think clearly as well.

UNLEASHING THE POWER OF OUR MINDS

When we can use all of these thinking tools effectively, we are well on our way to unleashing the power of our minds. Powerful minds lead individuals to reach for the stars, knowing that they have the thinking power to sustain them through their journey. Therefore, as young people or as adults, as students or professionals, regardless of our circumstances, we can apply these thinking tools, critical thinking strategies and habits of mind to our thinking process and be more effective in what we do.

CHAPTER 10 - FOOD FOR THOUGHT – USING OUR MINDS

TOPICS AND IDEAS FOR SELF-REFLECTION AND DISCUSSION

SELF-REFLECTION

"The mind is everything. What you think you become." Buddha

"Whatever the mind of man can conceive and believe, it can achieve." Napoleon Hill

"Above all else, guard your heart, for everything you do flows from it." Proverbs 4:23 (Bible)

GROUP DISCUSSION

This is a good place to do an analysis of the three statements above, and see in what ways they are similar. What do these different sayings mean? Why do you think they are important in their particular ages but also for people today?

CHAPTER 10 – REFERENCES AND FURTHER READING

Costa, A. L. (2021). What are Habits of Mind? The Institute for Habits of Mind. Available at *https://www. habitsofmindinstitute. org/about-us/hear-art/*

Fletcher, J. (2013). Critical Habits of Mind: Exposing the Process of Development. *Liberal Education, 99*(1), 1-5. Association of American Colleges & Universities: A Voice and a force for Liberal Education.

Mind Tools. Critical thinking" developing the right mindset and skills. Available at *https://www. mindtools. com/pages/article/newTED_95. htm*

CHAPTER 11

THINK BEFORE YOU ACT

To be a leader, you need to be in control of your actions. We all know that the power to think and use reason is our greatest asset. Yet, how many times have we had to ask ourselves, "How could I have done this?" and how many times have young people been rebuked by parents, rather unkindly at times, with "How could you have done such a silly thing?"

There's a simple explanation for this. We often do not stop to think before we respond or react. Adults are as guilty as young people and as children in this respect. The reason that we respond or react in a way that we find unreasonable later may be that we acted on impulse. Impulsive action is usually associated with animals or the immature. If we are to behave as the intelligent individuals that we are, if we are to be considered leaders and good examples, we must learn to curb our impulses.

IMPULSE OR REFLEX?

Some people boast about being able to act on impulse and they classify 'impulse' as 'reflex'. To be able to act on impulse, or to have good reflexes, is an advantage in moving out of harm's way, they may argue. However, many of the situations in which we act on impulse cannot be classified as harmful or even as potentially so, under normal conditions.

IMPULSIVENESS AND VIOLENCE

Yet, in many cases, by our impulsive actions, we convert a normal situation into a violent one. One person says something that another doesn't like, and the second person responds impulsively and in some instances with verbal abuse or physical violence. This may happen in a variety of situations: between spouses or partners, among siblings, between parents and children, and among children in the schoolyard or in public places. In more extreme situations, one individual, armed, responds impulsively to a taunt or a tease by another person, and lets fly a gunshot that results in another person's death. How senseless is that!

DIFFERENT DEFINITIONS OF IMPULSIVITY

What we have been speaking about is one definition of impulsivity, which involves acting without thinking things out. In this sense, it is acting without foresight. Impulsivity is a condition that is often seen among adolescents. Initially, impulsivity was thought to be caused by the immaturity of the adolescent brain, which was said to be not yet well developed (Steinberg & Chein, 2015).

However, with brain research over the years, it was discovered that there were increases in the volumes of the gray and white matter in the adolescent brain, making this brain function more efficiently and effectively than previously thought (Steinberg & Chein, 2015).

It was also hypothesized that impulsivity was not only related to immature cognitive control, but was accompanied by a temporary intensification of urges to pursue new and rewarding experiences. This theory became known as the "dual systems" or "maturational imbalance" theory, which held that adolescents tended to become more engaged in risk-taking because of this imbalance (Steinberg & Chein, 2015).

Several other explanations and causes have been associated with impulsivity. For example, some authors explain that sources of impulsivity can be found in fear, intoxication, medications, and may be associated with restlessness, inattention, and aggressiveness (Stoppler, 2021). Other causes of impulsivity have been identified as brain injury and neurodegenerative diseases, bipolar mania, ADHD, antisocial personality disorder (ASPD), as well as genetics (Salters-Pedneault, July 10, 2020).

Some authors take a broader and more comprehensive view of impulsivity, pointing out that it is associated with many psychiatric disorders, including addictions, attention deficit hyperactive disorder (ADHD), anti-social psychiatric disorder (ASPD), and genetics (Bevilacqua & Goldman, 2013).

MANIFESTATIONS VARY WIDELY

Many types of behaviours can become impulsive in people who have borderline personality disorders. These manifestations can include changing or cancelling plans abruptly, binge eating or drinking, escalating confrontations, frequently starting over things, having frequent emotional outbursts, quitting jobs suddenly, engaging in physical violence, and threatening others, to name a few (Salters-Pedneault, July 10, 2020). In short, manifestations involve behaviours that are impulsive in which the individual may not have put much forethought.

However, as one source notes, impulsivity can be seen in situations where acts "are well-planned but seemingly driven by a force that exceeds usual controls" (Schultz-Ross, 1999). In other words, although the acts may have been planned, they were not well thought out and hastily carried out. It is this latter meaning of impulsivity that needs serious attention. Individuals that find they are manifesting impulsivity of the second kind may need professional help to get over these conditions.

IMPULSIVITY, CONDITIONING AND INTERNET ADDICTION

Some researchers who have studied impulsivity among young people have pointed out that impulsivity can be a result of conditioning, as in the case of addictions. According to this thinking, impulsivity has been conditioned as some young people become addicted to the Internet. In this explanation, it is not implied that Internet use is a bad thing, but only that users addicted to its use may tend to seek out immediate gratification in other areas of their lives. This means that Internet addiction may be associated with impulsive tendencies, which discourage those addicted from thinking things out. As one researcher observes, "[a]nother construct that is related to internet overuse is impulsivity, which is understood as swift action without forethought or conscious judgment, behavior without adequate thought and the tendency to act with less forethought than do most individuals of equal ability and knowledge" (Chandiramani, 2014, p. 64). Being conscious of the possible connection between Internet addiction and impulsivity is enough to make some individuals think more seriously about their actions.

OTHER PSYCHIATRIC DISORDERS AND INTERNET ADDICTION

In another study on the relationship between Internet addiction and impulsivity, Cao and colleagues (2007) contend that while Internet addiction has been found to be associated with shyness, self-consciousness, loneliness, anxiety, depression and interpersonal challenges, that the finding of their research "suggests that adolescents with Internet addiction exhibit more impulsivity than controls and have various comorbid psychiatric disorders, which could be associated with the psychopathology of Internet addiction". From this study, many of the adolescents also had other psychiatric problems that may have predisposed them to Internet addiction (Cao, Su, Liu & Gao, 2007). Another study shows that Internet addiction is associated with 'poor impulse control' in much the same way as pathological gambling (Lee, Choi, Shin, Lee, Jung, & Kwon, 2012).

EARLY HELP

Some research studies point out that many children who experience impulsivity grow up to be teens and young adults who are impulsive, and who become disconnected from school and work. As pointed out, "Being disconnected during early ages (between sixteen and twenty-four) can have negative impacts on future labor-market success and other outcomes" (Loprest, Spaulding & Nightingale, 2019). Research on this group reveals that policies and programs, including education and training programs, can be used to engage and reengage these students to the world of school and work (Loprest et al. , 2019). While these measures can include individual programs, many community college systems and comprehensive services can help to target this group of impulsive and disconnected youth.

IMPULSIVITY CAN BE CONTROLLED

Measures can be used to control impulsivity. Where conditions are severe, treatment could be sought, either by parents of younger children and teens or by young adults. Seeking out professional help is greatly recommended.

TREATMENT AND COPING

While some cases of impulsivity warrant diagnosis of impairment of personality functioning, or impairment of interpersonal functioning, or of possible psychological or physical causes by professionals, treatment can often be achieved through psychotherapy and medication (Salters-Pedneault, July 10, 2020). Other cases of impulsivity may be controlled through using coping measures.

However, for impulsivity that may not be severe, professionals may even recommend that individuals use coping mechanisms. Even when individuals are using a treatment plan to deal with their impulsivity, there are steps recommended that can be taken to improve coping with impulsivity. According to Salters-Pedneault (July 10, 2020), some of the coping measures used are to "conduct a chain analysis" which allows the individual to identify his or her impulsive behavior and to note what happened before and afterwards; to "join a support group" for support in managing the impulsive behavior"; to "replace impulsive behaviours with healthy ones"; and to "practice deep breathing", which alleviates stress and helps to reduce impulsive behavior.

If in doubt as to whether your impulsive behavior is severe or not, you should seek out professional help, maybe starting with your personal physician or counsellor, who may then refer you to the right professional to deal with your impulsivity or any other condition that you may have.

LET'S THINK BEFORE WE ACT

Therefore, a good motto we should bear in mind is always to think before we act. Even when we may be tempted to act immediately without thinking through a challenge, let us be responsible leaders by taking time to think. By doing this, we may find that we save ourselves the embarrassment of doing something inappropriate.

CHAPTER 11 - FOOD FOR THOUGHT – THINK BEFORE YOU ACT

TOPICS AND IDEAS FOR SELF-REFLECTION AND DISCUSSION

SELF-REFLECTION

ASK YOURSELF:

"Am I an impulsive person?" "What kinds of things do I do?" "Have I ever gotten into trouble because of my impulsivity?" "How can I deal with this in the future?"

"Think before you act; think twice before you speak."
Thomas Browne

"Think before you do! Don't ever be in haste to make a mistake, for that can be a big mistake! Think before you do!" Ernest Agyemang Yeboah

GROUP DISCUSSION

Discuss this quote in your group meeting.

"Remember not only to say the right thing in the right place, but far more difficult still, to leave unsaid the wrong thing at the tempting moment."
Benjamin Franklin

Discuss strategies that people can use to curb their impulsivity.

What are some measures that teachers can use to help their students overcome impulsivity in the classroom?

Have you ever had to deal with impulsive people and how did it work out? If you face a similar situation today, how would you deal with it? What have you learned from this experience?

CHAPTER 11– REFERENCES AND FURTHER READING

Additude (Inside the ADHD mind). (June 18, 2020). Impulse control strategies for school and home. Available at *https://www. additudemag. com/impulse-control-strategies-adhd-students/*

Bevilacqua, L. & Goldman, D. (2013). Genetics of impulsive behavior. *Philosophical Transactions of the Royal Society B, 368 (20120380).*

Cao, F. , Su, L. , Liu, T. & Gao, X. (2007). The relationship between impulsivity and Internet addiction in a sample of Chinese adolescents. *European Psychiatry, 22*(7), 466-71.

Chandiramani, K. (2014). Internet addiction and impulsivity among adolescents. *Indian Journal of Health and Wellbeing, 5*(7), 64-67.

Lee, H. W. , Choi, J. , Shin, Y. , Lee, J. , Jung, H. Y. & Kwon, J. S. (2012). Impulsivity in internet addiction: a comparison with pathological gambling. *Cyberpsychology, Behavior, and Social Networking Journal,* 15(7), 373-377.

Loprest, P. , Spaulding, S. , & Nightingale, D. S. (2019). Disconnected young adults: Increasing engagement and opportunity: Improving employment and earnings in twenty-first century labor markets. *RSF: The Russell Sage Foundation Journal of the Social Sciences, 5*(5), 221-243.

Salters-Pedneault, K. (July 10, 2020). What is Impulsivity? Available at *https://www. verywellmind. com/impulsive-behavior-and-bpd-425483*

Schultz-Ross, R. A. (1999). Review of Christopher D. Webster and Margaret D. Jackson, eds. (1997). Impulsivity: Theory, Assessment and Treatment. New York: The Guilford Press. *American Journal of Psychotherapy, 53*(2), 261-262.

Shockness, I. (2019). *Preventing Dropout and Overcoming School Failure: 30 Ways for Older Teens and Young Adults to Achieve Academic Success.* Vanquest Publishing Inc. , 2020.

Steinberg, L. & Chein, M. (2015). Multiple accounts of adolescent impulsivity. *Proceedings of the National Academy of Sciences of the United States of America, 112*(29), 8807-8808.

CHAPTER 12

ALWAYS BE THERE AND BE ON TIME

If you are a young person just entering the work force for the first time, you would find that it is important to develop good work ethics. Going to work every day is part of what being a good employee is. More than that, it is important to develop the habit of getting to work on time. If you are a seasoned employee, you would also know the disadvantages of taking time off for being sick when you aren't really sick, and the jeopardy you pose to your job through frequent absences.

Some employees make it a habit of going to work late. "It just happens" is a common but honest expression by an employee who is late most times for work. "I get up with enough time, but at the last minute something goes wrong, and I leave the house five minutes later than I should. Then, I can't make my travel connections and I am late for work." Another usual explanation is: "The traffic was really heavy." While this may be true, the question that one may ask is, "Didn't you anticipate traffic?" Or one may also enquire, "Couldn't you have left with enough time to account for possible delays in traffic?"

SENDING THE WRONG MESSAGE?

When you are late, you are sending a message that being late is acceptable behavior in the particular establishment. When you take time off from work, you are saying that this work is boring, that you don't like your job, or that you may not even think of the job as being very important. Whether you are a long-time employee, or a very new one, whether you are working part-time or full-time, it is common courtesy to get to work on time and be there to take care of your responsibilities.

UNAVOIDABLE CIRCUMSTANCES

At times, unavoidable circumstances occur, and you are unable to get to work or to get to work on time. An example is when there is an accident, when the highway is completely blocked, and no one could get through. Or there are times when the subway may have stopped, and there is no way to get anywhere. There are also times when you would have personal crises and simply cannot go to work. These are all circumstances that could not have been anticipated under normal conditions. However, sleeping in late does not qualify as a crisis.

Some people believe that if you allocate adequate time to getting ready and reaching your destination on time, you would be seldom late. The rationale for this is that you would have anticipated possible normal delays that could occur, and would already have taken steps to deal with these.

CAN BE A DRAWBACK

Being late can be a drawback in all walks of life. Whether you are an employee, employer, self-employed person, student or friend, being late is inconsiderate to others. What you are actually saying when you are late for an appointment is that the other person is not as important as you are, and so he or she must wait for you.

LOSS OF RESPECT

Employers get angry and fire employees or deduct from the wages of employees who are habitually late. Employees who are always late also lose the respect of their employers and their co-workers. Self-employed people often experience loss of business for being late. Students could influence teachers negatively and could miss work because of lateness. Good friends could be very hurt when friends take them for granted, and keep them waiting, sometimes for hours.

LEAD BY EXAMPLE

Leaders are also expected to be punctual. In fact, according to Wagh (August 26, 2020), "Punctuality is very important in everyone's life" and it is "the exceptional quality of every great leader." Leaders must therefore be the examples for their followers, but this does not excuse followers from being punctual, even if their leaders are not good examples. As noted, punctuality shows respect and consideration for others. It identifies the individual employee as committed and willing to work, and as having a positive view of his or her workplace. In a classroom setting, punctuality shows respect for the teacher or professor and other classmates.

IS PUNCTUALITY A PROBLEM WITH MILLENNIALS?

Many people observe that millennials and young people in general tend to be late and that they may not be taking punctuality seriously. One author questions whether it is entitlement that leads to young people not showing up on time. "Twenty-something tardiness perhaps stems from the "entitled school of thought about our generation, the root cause of which could be quite different from older-generation tardiness" (Anglim, July 7, 2014). One possible reason, according to this author, is the availability of technology (smart phones) to call at the last minute and say one would be late a few minutes, or the feeling that one does not want to waste time waiting on another person, implying that one's time is more valuable than the other person's time .... This attitude is highly self-serving, inconsiderate, and downright rude" (Anglim, July 7, 2014).

GOOD ADVICE

If you are a young person, it is important that you develop the habit of being on time. Also, make it a habit to be at work every day, even if it is a part-time job or volunteer work. Be dependable. Employers are usually not tolerant with employees who arrive late for work or who skip days of work. Other employees also do not appreciate their tardy or absentee co-workers. When you are late, you are often not as organized and as effective as you can be. Anglim (July 7, 2014) points out, "In the professional world promptness should be taken even more seriously – and the stakes are higher for younger people." The word to the wise is that in the professional world, punctuality is even more critical for younger workers, so be on time.

CHAPTER 12 - FOOD FOR THOUGHT – ALWAYS BE THERE AND BE ON TIME

TOPICS AND IDEAS FOR SELF-REFLECTION AND DISCUSSION

SELF-REFLECTION

"Am I usually late?" "How can I fix this?" "What do I have to do so as not to be late?"

"Being on time to appointments and meetings is a phase of self-discipline and an evidence of self-respect. Punctuality is a courteous compliment the intelligent person pays to his associates." Marvin J. Ashton

"Arriving late was a way of saying that your own time was more valuable than the time of the person who waited for you. " Karen Joy Fowler

GROUP DISCUSSION

Discuss some of the reasons for the importance of punctuality. Recall occasions when you were late and when there may have been serious consequences.

You can also make a case for why you think punctuality is not important, if this is how you think.

You can play a punctuality game with your group. Be creative. One of the rules you can use is that members of the group who come late cannot play.

Your group can create and perform a skit where a prospective employee is late for an interview, or where an employee is late for work and the employer takes action.

CHAPTER 12– REFERENCES AND FURTHER READING

Anglim, A. (July 7, 2014). Are Twenty-Somethings Always Late for everything? LinkedIn. Available at *https://www. linkedin. com/pulse/20140707100950-92996947-are-twenty-somethings-always-late-for-everything*

Guskey, T. R, Swan, G. M. & Jung, L. A. (2011) GRADES that mean something. *The Phi Delta Kappan, 93*(2), 52-57

Munoz, M. A. & Guskey, T. R. (2015). Standards-based grading and reporting will improve education. *The Phi Delta Kappan, 96*(7), 64-68

Rahman, K. (2014). Towards responsible citizenry: Conceptual framework and the way forward. *Policy Perspectives, 11*(2), 93-117.

Wagh, S. (August 26, 2020). Punctuality: The exceptional quality of every leader. Available at *https://www. eatmy. news/2020/08/punctuality-exceptional-quality-of. html*

CHAPTER 13

BEING KIND AND CONSIDERATE TO OTHERS

In our busy world where size and show seem important, little things may seem insignificant, when in many instances, they aren't. How many times have we thought of doing something nice for someone, and decided against it, because of how others may think of us? Or maybe we thought we'd look simple, and not important, for showing that we care? How many times have we kept a stiff upper lip and tried to appear important, when it would have cost us nothing to smile at the person we just passed? And how many times have we cast that second glance that made someone feel uncomfortable, or made the other person feel that they did not belong or did not fit in? Sometimes, our actions may be quite innocent. How many times have we said a word that could have been misconstrued, and was, and how many times have we done something we thought insignificant, and it turned out to be very important to the other person?

UNFORGETTABLE EXPERIENCE

When I was about 11 or 12, I remember meeting an emotionally disturbed woman on the street. In fact, she was a teacher who had come to teach in our school district some time earlier, and who, reportedly because of a broken love affair, had tried to commit suicide on several occasions. She was hospitalized many times and each time she survived. She was back in our community once again after a hospitalization and people were saying that this last episode was a very close call.

Well, as I passed her on the street on a Friday afternoon after this last episode, I greeted her as I was expected to do. Living in a very small community, where everyone greeted everyone else, I said "hello" and she replied. But as I passed her, I looked back. To my dismay, she was also looking back, and, of course, I was so mortified because she saw me looking at her that I kept looking for a few more seconds. She kept looking at me intently until I turned away. I was embarrassed.

I remember experiencing a flood of emotions. I felt awful and for the whole weekend I could not put her stare out of my mind. Imagine my distress when I returned to school on Monday and discovered that she had taken her life that Friday night! I felt responsible. I thought if only I hadn't looked back!

As much as my parents comforted me then by telling me it wasn't my fault, I still felt guilty. In time, I came to think that even if I hadn't caused it, my looking back couldn't have helped, either. Over the years, ever so often I think about the incident, though I don't blame myself any more. I have accepted that this is the way things had to be.

WHEN A LITTLE MATTER MEANT A LOT

It has been quite some years I hadn't recalled this incident until some time ago, I read an article. It spoke of a young man, Steve (I don't remember his name), who recalled that when he was in junior high, there was a young boy who didn't really speak to anyone. Other students teased and bullied this boy. Anyway, one day as Steve was passing beside this boy's locker, he noticed that the boy had dropped a large pile of books. Steve bent down and helped him pick them up.

Steve never had any other dealing with this boy after that, and he barely remembered the boy's name.

Several years later, Steve explained that in some public place, probably a mall, a young man addressed him in a very familiar way. When Steve turned around, he recognized the young man. This was the boy who had spilled his books that morning in junior high. Steve was a little taken aback, because he was not really friends with this boy. But from the manner in which this young man had greeted him, Steve realized that anyone would have thought they had been best buddies who had been separated for some time. Steve reciprocated the familiarity so as not to embarrass this young man.

Then the young man told Steve his story. That morning, several years earlier, when Steve had bent down to help him (as a young boy) pick up the books he had dropped, he was cleaning out his locker and was getting ready to take his books home. He was doing this, in preparation for the suicide he had planned to commit that night. He explained to Steve that he didn't want to worry his mother with having to clean out his locker after he was gone.

The young man told Steve that after Steve had stopped to help him that morning, he felt that he had a friend, and so changed his mind about taking his life. When Steve had helped him pick up his books, it was only a little thing and Steve didn't think that it mattered, but it did.

PAY ATTENTION TO THE LITTLE THINGS

As we go to work, to school, or wherever we have contact with others, let us think about the impact our actions could have on others. Think about the little things that we do, sometimes unconsciously, which could have such a dramatic effect on the lives of other people! Think of the nice things that we can do or say that can make someone's day and ours a little less difficult!

This is an important way in which we can be leaders, for in being nice to someone we could spur that person on to be nice to others, and we can start a cycle that could continue for the whole day, and even longer. Remember, the people to whom we are kind need not be kind to us in return. It was John Bunyan in Pilgrim Progress who noted: "You have not lived today until you have done something for someone who can never repay you."

CHAPTER 13 - FOOD FOR THOUGHT – BEING KIND AND CONSIDERATE TO OTHERS

TOPICS AND IDEAS FOR SELF-REFLECTION AND DISCUSSION

SELF-REFLECTION

Think of the little things you can do to make life easier for those around you, whether at home, at school, or in your community.

"You cannot do a kindness too soon, for you never know how soon it will be too late." Ralph Waldo Emerson

"Too often we underestimate the power of a touch, a smile, a kind word, a listening ear, an honest compliment, or the smallest act of caring, all of which have the potential to turn a life around." Leo Buscaglia

"A warm smile is the universal language of kindness." William Arthur Ward

"I expect to pass through this world but once. Any good therefore that I can do, or any kindness that I can show to my fellow-creature, let me do it now. Let me not defer or neglect it, for I shall not pass this way again."

William Penn

GROUP DISCUSSION

"Happiness is the new rich. Inner peace is the new success. Health is the new wealth. Kindness is the new cool." Syed Balkhi

This can be the theme of a discussion for your group one evening. Groups can be broken down into four, with each subgroup taking one of these statements. Then the four subgroups merge again and join in discussion. The whole quote could be a discussion for all members of the group participating. For teachers or instructors, this could be the basis for a post from your students.

"Successful people are always looking for opportunities to help others. Unsuccessful people are always asking "What's in it for me?" Brian Tracy

Are there any community activities that your group can engage in that will make a difference to the homelessness, hunger, or climate change situation in your community?

Do you have ideas that could help? Does anyone in the group have an idea of making a difference? As President John F. Kennedy once remarked: *"One person can make a difference, and everyone should try."* Will your group support such a person or persons?

CHAPTER 13– REFERENCES AND FURTHER READING

Hall, K. (December 4, 2017). The importance of kindness: Being kind can strengthen your relationships and sense of satisfaction in life. Psychology Today. Available at *https://www.psychologytoday. com/ca/blog/pieces-mind/201712/the-importance-kindness*

Nazareno, L. & Krafel, A. (March 2017). Taking care of ourselves and others. *The Phi Delta Kappan, 98*(6), 25-30.

Sharma, N. (November 1, 2018). Why should we be kind to others? Kindness provides many benefits to a human being and below is a list of these benefits explained in a bit more detail. Available at Thrive Global at *https://thriveglobal.com/stories/why-should-we-be-kind-to-others/*

CHAPTER 14

BEWARE OF INDUCEMENTS

As a leader, be aware and beware of inducements. In recent days, we have been hearing of young people being induced with promises of adventure and excitement to leave home. We may argue that those who induce young people to leave home, particularly adults, should be severely punished and even prosecuted. This is considered appropriate punishment. Every day, however, there are many young people who are being induced by others to do things that may be considered inappropriate, illegal, or simply wrong.

YOU HAVE A MIND OF YOUR OWN

As a young person, you have to start thinking of yourself as someone who has a mind of your own. You have to start thinking for yourself. If you are a young person, beware of inducements to become involved in activities that will produce adventure and excitement that you know are wrong or even criminal. If you are a young person, you have to start taking responsibility for your actions and for what happens to you. This is the time for you to try out those skills that you need to develop as you move into adulthood.

DON'T BLAME FRIENDS

In the first place, good things do not come easy. If you are to excel in school, you have to study. If you allow yourself to be influenced not to study, then you are responsible for not studying and for not knowing your work. You cannot blame friends for your academic failure.

WRONG THINGS CAN NEVER BE RIGHT

Secondly, wrong things could never be considered right. You know that certain actions are wrong. If you steal or tell a lie, you know you are doing wrong. The fact that someone may have encouraged you to do so does not free you from your responsibility to do what is right.

FACE YOUR DIFFICULT SITUATION

Thirdly, if you are facing a difficult situation, the answer does not necessarily entail your running away from it. You should address the situation and deal with it. If you need help to analyze the situation more objectively, ask a responsible adult to help you. Seeking adventure and excitement does not rid you of a problem. It may be a temporary relief, because for a while, sometimes for a very short while, you may forget about your pressing problem.

INDUCED BY PROMISES OF MONEY AND FAME?

You may be induced with large sums of money by adults or other young people who promise you fame and adventure. If you are unemployed or have no prospects of employment, this may seem as an attractive inducement. You may reason that you will become involved for only a short period of time, until you are over whatever problem you may have. As usually happens, though, when someone becomes involved in certain activities, it becomes very difficult, and sometimes impossible, to break free, without severe consequences. In many instances, whatever gains may have been made in the short term cannot compensate for the great loss experienced or that would be experienced in the long term.

PROMISES FALL SHORT

However, in many instances, the activity that promises to give you adventure and excitement falls short and may have consequences of its own. The result may be that you not only still have your original problem, but you may have new problems as well, sometimes even more serious than your original problem.

A WORD OF CAUTION

Do not be induced by others, whether adults or other young people, to do things you know are wrong, questionable, or even criminal. The fact that you find something questionable is usually an indication that you know it is wrong, and that you are looking for some way of convincing yourself that it is right. There are many young people now who are in trouble with the law, with their parents and with others, because they listened to the inducements of others.

INDUCEMENTS CAN BE UNREASONABLE

Often, inducements are unreasonable. You know there is no right way you could get something expensive if you do not have a job paying you a lot of money, or if you do not have the money. You know there is no way you could afford to live on your own in a city if you do not have the money to pay for accommodation. You know if you are a young person, below the legal age of working, or without marketable skills, it would be close to impossible to support yourself by working. Living on the streets really doesn't make sense, when you consider you have no family to care for you, and you have no way of supporting yourself. There is no right way of running away from home and being on your own, without having a place to stay or money for food. Right from the outset, you know a proposition such as this makes absolutely no sense.

DO THE RIGHT THING

You know when something is wrong. Do the right thing. Walk away from inducements of money. If you didn't work for something, or you weren't given it as a gift by a close family member, then you should not consider it yours. Walk away from inducements of adventure and excitement. You know in your heart that certain inducements are wrong and may carry heavy consequences, if you are caught. You may be thinking that you are under 18, and you could get away with breaking the law. You may think the consequences may be quite light as a young or juvenile offender. But don't count on it. You may find that in the long run your self-esteem and self-respect could be damaged beyond repair, not to mention other aspects of your life. Life could be very difficult for you for a very long time.

LET'S BE REAL

No one gives you money for nothing. You may find out later the money comes with many strings attached. Don't be fooled. Don't fall for inducements, because you may discover that the emotional, social and legal costs are just too great. Be a leader. Stand up to inducements. Turn them down. Show that you are capable of thinking for yourself and that you can make good and sound decisions.

CHAPTER 14 - FOOD FOR THOUGHT – BEWARE OF INDUCEMENTS

TOPICS AND IDEAS FOR SELF-REFLECTION AND DISCUSSION

SELF-REFLECTION

"Have the courage to say no. Have the courage to face the truth. Do the right thing because it is right. These are the magic keys to living your life with integrity." (W. Clement Stone)

GROUP DISCUSSION

Discuss ways that young people could protect themselves against those who would try to induce them to do the wrong things.

Discuss places where some unscrupulous individuals reach out to young people and some circumstances that would lead young people into situations where they fall victim to exploitation?

What are some organizations within your community that reach out to help young people who have been victimized, such as being trafficked or exploited in other ways?

CHAPTER 14– REFERENCES AND FURTHER READING

Changing Minds (n. d.). Persuasion, inducement and coercion. Available at _http://changingminds._ _org/techniques/general/articles/persuasion_inducement_coerci_ _on. htm_

Helping People take Responsibility: what does it mean to take ownership of your work. Mind Tools. Available at _https://www. mindtools. com/pages/article/taking-_ _responsibility. htm_

CHAPTER 15

WHEN THINGS GO WRONG . . . AS THEY SOMETIMES DO

Usually, when we do something wrong or make a mistake, we may try to avoid taking responsibility. But taking responsibility often leads to a better outcome. Good leaders take responsibility for their actions, admit when they are wrong and help speed the process of putting things right. This is a practice that often works well, whether or not we serve in an official capacity as leader.

DON'T BLAME OTHERS

When we panic, we fall into confusion, and we are unable to think clearly. As we panic, we think of the things that we should have done, and we express regret, frustration and anger. We become anxious, because we become preoccupied with the situation that we are in, and that is all we can see. In our frantic state, we catch at anything that would give us relief, and so we start looking for places to lay blame. We more often than not find someone or something to blame. In the unusual circumstance, or when we run out of places to assign blame, we blame ourselves, but could quickly add that the reason we are to blame is that we had no other choice.

A TYPICAL SCENARIO

Fifteen-year-old Sondra decided to go out with her friends after school. She did not tell her mother about this beforehand, because her friends only made the decision to go out while they were at school. Sondra knew that if she asked, she would be told "No," and she wanted to be part of the group. She decided to go, especially after Kelly explained to her how much fun it would be. Sondra went with Kelly and her friends in one car.

GETTING ANXIOUS

Later, at about seven in the evening, Sondra started getting anxious, because she did not even call her mother to let her know where she was. Sondra's mother kept calling Sondra's cell phone, but Sondra did not answer. Sondra's mother only knew Sondra' friend, Kelly, but did not have Kelly's phone number. Needless to say, Sondra's mother was worried, and Sondra knew that. Sondra began panicking. She asked Kelly to take her home, but Kelly wanted to stay and so refused. Since Sondra had no transportation and no money, she decided to wait until her friends were ready to leave. Sondra worried so much while she was out that she did not have the fun that Kelly had promised. Sondra worried about what her mother would do, when she found out what Sondra had done.

MOTHER FURIOUS

When Sondra got home at 9:35 that evening, her mother was furious. Sondra tried to explain what had happened. It didn't help much for she got grounded anyway. In her panic and anxiety, Sondra started looking for someone or something to blame. In her despair, Sondra tried to blame everyone, except herself. She blamed Kelly for encouraging her. She blamed her friends for staying out very late. She blamed her mother for being too strict and for being very hard on her. She blamed her mother for not giving her money. If only she had bus fare, Sondra rationalized, she would have left. She blamed everyone, except herself.

PAB

What Sondra had done so far was entertain PAB: Panic, Anxiety, and Blame. She had done all the wrong things, because none of these could have helped the situation. In the first place, when she was confronted with the temptation to go out with friends, she should have said "No." Next, even if she had made the decision, had gone out with her friends and found herself in this predicament, she would have been better off thinking clearly, and trying to find a solution. Also, she could possibly have borrowed money from Kelly to take the bus home. Lastly, she could also have answered her phone or called her mother and explained what had happened. She knew ahead of time that she was going to be punished.

FINDING A SOLUTION NEEDS A CLEAR MIND

In order to look for the solution to a problem, you must have a clear mind. Think about the problem, and break it down into its component parts. Look at the possible solutions, and then choose the most practical one. Had Sondra chosen to call her mother and explain the situation, she would very likely have been punished for going out without first getting permission, but things could have turned out to be less complicated than they did.

CHAPTER 15 - FOOD FOR THOUGHT – WHEN THINGS GO WRONG . . . AS THEY SOMETIMES DO

TOPICS AND IDEAS FOR SELF-REFLECTION AND DISCUSSION

SELF-REFLECTION

Accept responsibility and try to find a solution.

Also, accept responsibility and build trust.

"You can make mistakes, but you aren't a failure until you start blaming others for those mistakes" (John Wooden)

GROUP DISCUSSION

Discuss ways that people could try to shirk their responsibilities and blame others.

Think of situations that you may have shirked your responsibility and blamed others for mistakes that you have made. (Are you willing to discuss this in a group and take responsibility?"

Think of ways of reversing this behavior of blaming others for your mistakes, and think of ways you can start accepting responsibility and absolving others of blame.

Can you go back and reverse a situation where you shirked your responsibility and blamed others for your mistakes?

CHAPTER 15– REFERENCES AND FURTHER READING

Clemmer, J. (2021). Leaders take responsibility for their choices. The Clemmer Group. Available at *https://www. clemmergroup. com/articles/leaders-take-responsibility-choices/*

Lozano, E. B. & Laurent, S. M. (2019). The effect of admitting fault versus shifting blame on expectations for others to do the same. PLOS ONE, 14(3):e0213276. *https://doi. org/10. 1371/journal. pone. 0213276*

CHAPTER 16

DON'T QUIT ON YOURSELF – TURN YOUR LIFE AROUND

When life seems to be going in the wrong direction and nothing seems to be working out, this is the time to take stock and make the decision to change. This usually means being very honest with yourself and taking as objective a view of things as you could. It is time to stop and take a serious look at what you are doing, what is not working the way you intended, and what is causing the most difficulty in your life. You may even enlist the help of a close friend, who could be honest with you and tell you not what you want to hear, but what you need to hear.

NEVER TOO LATE TO CHANGE

Once you collect as much data as possible about yourself, use it to make changes. Although you may have been going the wrong way and doing the wrong things for a long time, it is never too late to make changes. If you are a young person who is in a behavioral class at school or who is getting into fights and arguments with our classmates, you could very well turn things around. If you are continually being reprimanded at home and at school for something that you are doing, then maybe it is time to take a serious look at your actions. If you are frequently being suspended or have been expelled from school for certain behavior, it is time you pay attention to the behavior that is causing this response. Try to think why you may be doing the things that are getting you into trouble. Try to see how these things are causing problems, and think of ways you can change these things.

SPEAK ABOUT WHAT'S BOTHERING YOU, IF ANYTHING

You may not know what is causing the problems. You may need help here. If there is something bothering you, speak about it. Talk to your parents. If you cannot or do not want to speak to them, speak to your guidance counsellor at school, a social worker or other professional. These professionals are there to help you during your difficult times. They will either help you or get you the resources that would provide you with the help that you need.

If you are a victim of physical, emotional, or sexual abuse, you have to speak up now and get help and counselling. The longer you wait, the more difficult the situation could become, and the more damage can be done. If you are an abuser, get help also, for it is never too late to change things. It may be embarrassing or even costly professionally to do so, but it is better to face up to your shortcomings now, get help, and change things now for you and for those that you abuse.

ANGER PROBLEMS?

If you have a problem with anger, that is, if you get angry at the slightest inconvenience, you need to speak to your school counsellor or social worker. There are programs that deal specifically with managing anger, and these professionals could get you into one of these programs or provide you with individual assistance. Having unmanageable anger or bursting into fits of rage at the slightest provocation is very dangerous for you and for others around you.

ANGER PROBLEMS SOMETIMES CONNECTED TO DRUG USE

Research shows that many young people who have problems with anger often have substance abuse issues. If you are presently using alcohol or other drugs and believe you can stop whenever you want, think again. Even cigarettes can be addictive.

Think how much more addictive drugs like cocaine, heroin, and ecstasy can be and the damage they could cause. Or maybe you are trying out new designer drugs. Think of the great risk you are taking when you use these drugs. There is no guarantee that these drugs are safe and no control over their quality or content. Some young people have actually overdosed after ingesting or inhaling illegal drugs they purchased from a dealer or online. Don't be fooled. If you have just started experimenting with alcohol or other drugs, or are a long-time user, it is time to make a change.

MANY SOURCES OF HELP

Regardless of the city in which you live, you could get information from many sources, for example, a school guidance counsellor if you are still a student at school. If you are out of school, and have substance abuse problems, you could speak to your doctor or any doctor for that matter. You may also speak to a youth pastor or religious leader, who may be able to refer you to facilities that can help you. There may be a walk-in clinic in your area or independent groups operating in your community that could help you with any of these difficult areas in your life. Look for help if you have a problem, since problems seldom disappear without attention. The longer you wait, the worst off the situation could become.

IN TROUBLE WITH THE LAW?

If you are in trouble with the law, all is not lost. You may have messed up, but you are the only person that could make the decision to turn your life around. Judge Greg Mathis, who as a young boy fell in with bad company and did time in juvenile detention, came to the decision one day to turn his life around. Reportedly, as his mother told him she was going to die, he promised her he would change his behavior. He did. Mathis grew up keeping his promise to his mother. His biography revealed that after becoming a judge in Chicago, he spent (and probably still does spend) a great deal of time trying to reach out to young people who need to turn their lives around. If you are a young person in trouble with the law, you could also make the most important decision today and make a change in your life. If this is your decision and you are not quite sure how to go about it, tell a trusted adult about your decision to change and ask for their help.

CHAPTER 16 - FOOD FOR THOUGHT – DON'T QUIT ON YOURSELF – TURN YOUR LIFE AROUND

TOPICS AND IDEAS FOR SELF-REFLECTION AND DISCUSSION

SELF-REFLECTION

Look below at what all of these individuals are saying about not quitting on yourself. It is not only one person who sees this idea of staying on when things seem very bleak as the way to go. Several of these individuals in different walks of life encourage you to stick with it and come out successful in the end.

"You may encounter many defeats, but you must not be defeated. In fact, it may be necessary to encounter the defeats, so you can know who you are, what you can rise from, how you can still come out of it." Maya Angelou

"Being defeated is often a temporary condition. Giving up is what makes it permanent." Marilyn Vos Savant

Success seems to be connected with action. Successful people keep

moving. They make mistakes, but they don't quit. - Conrad Hilton

"Winners never quit and quitters never win!" Vince Lombardi

"All our dreams can come true – if we have the courage to pursue them." Walt Disney

"Many of life's failures are people who did not realize how close they were to success when they gave up." Thomas Edison

All of these people encourage you to hold on, don't quit, and see any setbacks or failures as only a catalyst for moving ahead. You are on the right track now.

GROUP DISCUSSION

Make these quotes the subject of group discussions. Have group members say how they see these relating to their lives or the lives of other young people.

"Success is to be measured not so much by the position that one has reached in life as by the obstacles which he (she) has overcome while trying to succeed." Booker T. Washington

"The power of can't: The word 'can't' makes strong people weak, blinds people who can see, saddens happy people, turns brave people into cowards, robs a genius of their brilliance, causes rich people to think poorly, and limits the achievements of that great person living inside us all." Robert T. Kiyosaki

Learn these quotes. Make them part of your everyday life. Say them every day until they make up the very fibre of your being. When difficulties present themselves, just recite one of these quotes.

Young people may quit on many different aspects of their lives. What are some of these areas and what measures can they take to turn their lives around? How can friends help friends who want to quit on themselves?

CHAPTER 16 – REFERENCES AND FURTHER READING

Choenni, V. , Hammink, A. , & Van de Mheen, D. (2017). Association between Substance Use and the Perpetration of Family Violence in Industrialized Countries: A Systematic Review. *Trauma, Violence & Abuse, 18*(1), 37-50. doi:10. 2307/26638160

Eliot-Engel, J. & Westfall-Rudd. D. (2016). What is a culturally-responsible educator? *The Agricultural Education Magazine, 89*(2), 1-5

Ferguson, K. , Bender, K. , & Thompson, S. (2014). Social Estrangement Factors Associated with Income Generation Among Homeless Young Adults in Three U. S. Cities. *Journal of the Society for Social Work and Research, 5*(4), 461-487. doi:10. 1086/678921

Mackin, J. (1999). From boot camp to monastery. *Human Ecology Forum, 27*(1), 1-7

Mathis, G. (2002). *Inner City Miracle.* New York: Ballantine Books.

Reyes, J. (2012). How children succeed: Grit, curiosity, and the hidden power of character. *Journal of Research in Character Education, 10*(1), 1-4.

Williams, J. (2011). Help families by fostering parental involvement. Show an interest in your students' families before demanding that parents support your school. *Phi Delta Kappan, 93*(3), 1-5.

CHAPTER 17

GETTING "UNSTUCK" THROUGH POSITIVE AFFIRMATIONS

When I was about nineteen, I listened to a motivational speaker who explained that our minds could only process the images we provide. I did not fully grasp the meaning of what he was saying, especially as I thought of the word 'affirmation' as being only positive. Nevertheless, the illustrations he used remained with me and it was not until several years later that I truly understood the significance of 'positive affirmation'.

POSITIVE AND NEGATIVE?

When we affirm, we declare something to be true. We could affirm something positive or something negative. We could affirm that we are striving to be good and to be successful, which is a positive affirmation, or we could affirm that we are striving not to fail, which is a negative affirmation. I did not understand this distinction at first, because both statements suggested to me a desire for improvement.

DOESN'T ACKNOWLEDGE 'NOT'

However, as the motivational speaker explained, in the first case, the image that we present to our minds when we think of ourselves striving to succeed is positive, because the image that is presented is that of us succeeding. In the second case, where we are striving not to fail, the image that we present to our minds is that of us not failing. Our minds do not acknowledge the concept 'not' and so the image that our minds accept under these circumstances is that of failing.

STRESS NEGATIVE - NO

One of the illustrations this speaker used, and which was to impact me later, was that of a waiter and waitress thinking of serving guests at a large convention. The waiter affirmed that he would not make a mistake or trip and spill coffee all over the guests. He wanted to be sure that he did nothing wrong that night. Therefore, for the week leading up to the convention, all he could think about was not making a mistake and not spilling anything. On the night of the convention, the waiter was so focused on not spilling anything that he spilled a tray of drinks on one of the guests. The image he was presenting to his mind all week was that of 'spilling,' which was exactly what he did not want to do. This is an example of negative affirmation.

STRESS POSITIVE - YES

On the other hand, prior to the convention the waitress had been thinking about giving her best performance, serving her guests politely and promptly, and proving that she was the best waitress there. Her affirmations were positive because she saw herself succeeding. She was successful for the evening as everything went as planned. Had the waiter affirmed his success, he would most likely have been successful.

MUST FOCUS ON THE POSITIVE

The difference between these two individuals, as the motivational speaker explained, was that one focused on negative affirmations, while the other focused on positive ones. Their minds picked up the images that they presented and helped them perform according to the images that they had of themselves.

WE ARE WHAT WE THINK

Other writers and researchers support this concept, though presenting it in slightly different ways. Yet, what it boils down to is that "we are what we think", as Clement Stone, another motivational speaker, points out. Others present a similar concept in the idea of visualization. If we could think of ourselves doing the things in which we want to succeed, invariably we would succeed. There is a story of a prisoner of war who, in his isolation, imagined himself playing holes of golf. On his release from captivity several years later, he turned out to be an exceptionally good golfer, because of the practice he had engaged in through visualization while in captivity.

LAW OF ATTRACTION

Today, this idea of positive affirmations is firmly planted in the concept of Law of Attraction. This is a concept that encourages you to attract wealth, health and all the good things in life by thinking positively about them.

POWERFUL MINDS

What this tells us is that our minds are very powerful, and that the images and messages that we present to our minds or what we think about have the power to translate into performance. So give yourself positive affirmations and see yourself succeed. Be the leader who continues to stress positive affirmations for you and the others you influence.

CHAPTER 17 - FOOD FOR THOUGHT – GETTING "UNSTUCK" THROUGH POSITIVE AFFIRMATIONS

TOPICS AND IDEAS FOR SELF-REFLECTION AND DISCUSSION

SELF-REFLECTION

("What are some positive affirmations I can give myself on a daily basis to improve my performance?) – Make a list and consult it every day.

GROUP DISCUSSION

Why are positive affirmations so important?

Think of different situations where people need to perform well, and provide some of the positive affirmations they can give to themselves.

CHAPTER 17– REFERENCES AND FURTHER READING

Canfield, J. (2010). Key to Living the Law of Attraction: A Simple Guide to Creating the Life of Your Dreams. Health Communications.

Hill, N. (n. d.). The Strangest Secret. Available as articles at *https://www. nightingale. com/articles/the-strangest-secret/*

Hill, N. (2005 edition). Think and Grow Rich. TarcherPerigee, Publisher. Stone, C. & Hill, N. (2007). Success through a Positive Mental Attitude. Gallery Books

What is the Law of Attraction? Open Your Eyes to a World of Endless Possibilities. Available at *https://www. thelawofattraction. com/what-is-the-law-of-attraction/*

CHAPTER 18

WHEN HALF-HEARTED COMPLIMENTS IMPLY FAILURE

There is criticism that implies failure. Someone may have drawn a finely detailed portrait, one that looked fine. Instead of acknowledging the quality of his work, we begrudged giving him credit. When we looked at the portrait, instead of saying "What intricate work you have done!" we implied from our words and the tone of our voices that there may have been something wrong with the portrait. We may also have asked, "Where did YOU learn to draw?" If that individual was really confident in his abilities, our words and tone may not have mattered very much. That person may have revealed that his portrait was based on a skill he picked up and which he developed without benefit of instruction.

BE ENCOURAGING

On the other hand, if that individual was not self-confident, and was in need of some positive reinforcement, that person may have responded to us, "Doesn't it look good?" We could then have continued with our negativity by saying, "Yeah! It's O. K." That individual may then have enquired, "Just O. K.?" , and begrudgingly we may have replied, "Yeah, it's O. K." That individual may have gathered from our tone that there was something lacking in his work, or that the work was no good. This young person could have been easily discouraged when in fact he had the potential to do even greater work. In some cases, jealousy may have prevailed and prevented us from truly acknowledging this person's talent.

BE KIND

Had we reacted differently, we could have made the world of difference. "You have done excellent detail here! This is remarkable." The other person's response may have been, "You think so?" We may have replied, "Sure!" If we thought that the person could have benefitted from more direction or instruction, we could have simply asked, "Have you ever thought of pursuing this further?" In this case, we would have communicated to that young person that his work was exceptional, that he had talent, and that with further instruction or guidance he could accomplish even greater works.

WHEN CRITICISM IS IN PLACE

There are occasions, though, when a person does a remarkable work, and there are areas in the work that can be improved. Criticism may be in place. However, what is important is how that criticism is given. It could be a friendly nudge that if something were done a little differently, the work would be even more outstanding. However, if criticism was not solicited, it may not be appropriate to give it. Also, some young people have difficulty taking criticism from parents, maybe because of the tone in which the criticism may be given. Therefore, parents must be aware of giving criticism when such was not solicited. Even when criticism is solicited, it would depend on the relationship between the parent and the young person, as well as on how accepting the young person is to criticism.

GIVE CREDIT WHERE CREDIT IS DUE

I have seen young people discouraged simply because others that they cared about were unwilling to give credit where credit was due. No one is perfect, and a young person is not expected to know everything there is about something. No one is. In fact, we are learning new things every day, and becoming better at what we do.

PARALYZING OR CRYSTALLIZING

Therefore, if you are an adult or a young person, before you criticize other people on their accomplishments, think about the effect your criticism could have. Look for what is good in what they have done, rather than what is bad or lacking. Look at what they have accomplished, rather than what they haven't. Ask yourself, "Will my criticism discourage this individual or encourage him or her?" "Will my criticism cause a "paralyzing experience" or a "crystallizing" one?" "Will my criticism cause this young person to give up or would it empower him or her to try even harder?" Lean to the side of encouragement rather than to that of discouragement.

HAVE CONFIDENCE IN YOUR ABILITIES

If you are a young person with a talent, or if you are trying to develop a skill, don't be discouraged by half-hearted compliments. Have confidence in your abilities and seek professional instruction wherever possible. The more you learn, the more confidence you'll develop. Also, it takes time to develop a talent or skill, and there is always room for improvement and the opportunity to learn something new. Be always ready for constructive criticism and do not take it as a rejection of your work. Keep an open mind. Remember, too, it takes time to really learn a skill well, but once you have developed it, it's for life.

CHAPTER 18 - FOOD FOR THOUGHT – WHEN HALF-HEARTED COMPLIMENTS IMPLY FAILURE

TOPICS AND IDEAS FOR SELF-REFLECTION AND DISCUSSION

SELF-REFLECTION

Think about these quotes:

"Whatever the mind can conceive and believe, it can achieve." Napoleon Hill

Equip yourself with positive thinking and you will soon find that things start going your way.

"If you think you can, or you think you can't, you're probably right."
Henry Ford

GROUP DISCUSSION

Discuss how compliments could be given heart-heartedly and show how this could have a negative impact on those receiving the compliments.

Discuss ways of how individuals could provide genuine compliments to others and how these compliments could help.

Undertake creative activities and encourage group members to encourage each other.

CHAPTER 18– REFERENCES AND FURTHER READING

Moss, W. , & Moses, D. (2018). Confidence: How to build the skills (not just bravado). In *Raising Independent, Self-Confident Kids: Nine Essential Skills to Teach Your Child or Teen* (pp. 33-56). Washington, DC: American Psychological Association.

Room for improvement: Compliments first or bad news first? Available at *https://www. newscientist. com/lastword/mg24532711-500-room-for-improvement-compliment-first-or-bad-news-first/*

Silvey, P. E. (2014). Reducing Apprehensions of Adolescent Singers in Choral Classrooms. *Music Educators Journal, 100*(3), 53-59.

CHAPTER 19

WHEN COMPLIMENTS CAN BE DISCOURAGING

Positive criticism is often encouraging and often leads to improvement. Negative criticism is usually discouraging, although when it is given and taken in the right spirit, it could encourage and lead to greater things. 'Positive criticism' or a compliment that is given half-heartedly is usually no better than 'negative criticism' given in the wrong spirit.

We normally give positive criticism or evaluation of a work or a behavior when that work or behavior meets our approval, or when others identify the work or the behavior as adequate or appropriate. We give negative criticism when something does not meet our approval, and this could be in terms of quality of work or in terms of our own taste. We may judge a certain behavior as inappropriate for one occasion and criticize it negatively, although we may find that same behavior displayed in a different situation appropriate and desirable.

HALF-HEARTED COMPLIMENTS

However, there is positive criticism that can be given half-heartedly, and this could be discouraging. As a young person, I was invited to spend a weekend with a girlfriend. Things were going fine until another girl dropped in unexpectedly. We continued what we were doing, and my friend tried on a new outfit and asked our opinions. "How does this look?" It looked great, but even before I could have made a comment, the other girl blurted out, "I have seen worse," possibly as a joke. This response led to my friend taking off the outfit immediately. As it turned out, this was the outfit that my friend had liked best. Although the girl tried later to convince my friend that my friend's outfit looked great, because it did, the fact that she had given a half-hearted response so impulsively in the first place destroyed any opportunity of our convincing my friend that her outfit was fine. My friend eventually gave the outfit to her younger sister. In retrospect, I realize that my friend was quite insecure. It goes to show that when we give positive criticism or compliment, we should make sure that it has a positive effect.

DISCOURAGED WITH ELEMENT OF DOUBT

In another instance that took place a few years ago, I was invited to a celebration at a friend's house. My friend's teenage son, Ezra, was very interested in art and taught himself to draw from books he had borrowed from the library. His mother was very proud of him. She had framed some of his drawings and displayed them on her living room walls. At this function, I overheard a conversation between Ezra and another boy, in which the other boy was commenting on Ezra's drawings." I guess they are O. K. , but what else do you do?" It was obvious that Ezra expected a more positive response from his friend, but this was not forthcoming. Although his friend gave what appeared as positive criticism, there was an element of doubt that could have been discouraging.

This one event cannot be held responsible for the fact that Ezra has since given up drawing, his love for five years, but it is this kind of half-hearted compliment that could be discouraging.

ACKNOWLEDGE ACHIEVEMENT

Criticizing how our friends look and what they do should be something we do with kindness and consideration, if we do it at all. Rather than saying something like, "You really outdid yourself," "That's great," "What an accomplishment," when our friends have done something outstanding, we may try to downplay their success. We may do this by pointing out some greater accomplishment we may have had, something that may stand out more than our friend's achievement. For example, in response to a friend's comment that she received an award as 'student of the month', a friend may imply that there was nothing exceptional about this, considering that she had just made the dean's list. It is important to know when to acknowledge a friend's success and let that stand on its own merit. There will be another time for sharing one's good news.

NOT DETRACTING FROM YOUR ACCOMPLISHMENTS

Giving a compliment to someone who has accomplished something great should not be seen as detracting from what we ourselves have accomplished, so we should not begrudge giving that compliment. At the same time, when we give negative criticism, we should consider the impact of what we have to say. Will our words discourage the other person, or encourage him or her to make changes and improve, if changes need to be made? We must realize that if the other person values our opinion, then we must be careful what we say and how we say it. If there is need for improvement, we need to say it, but we must be kind and tactful in how we do so.

POSITIVE CRITICISM SHOULD HAVE POSITIVE EFFECT

A positive criticism should have a positive effect. When we give half-hearted compliments, we are saying either, "What you are doing doesn't really look good but we are only complimenting you so as not to embarrass you," or that "What you are doing really looks good, but we begrudge making you feel proud of yourself." Unfortunately, some people receiving these half-hearted compliments sometimes cannot decipher which meaning to attach to it.

In this way, they may become discouraged, and may choose to abandon a path that may have led to greatness. They lose out because of our half-hearted positive criticism or compliment. However, when this happens, we lose, too. For remember, what is lost to one of us is lost to all, and what is gained by one enriches us all.

BE A LEADER

Be a leader. Set the tone among your friends. Be supportive of their efforts and encourage them. Compliment them on their achievements. Their success does not diminish yours. They, in turn, will encourage others, including you.

CHAPTER 19 - FOOD FOR THOUGHT – WHEN COMPLIMENTS CAN BE DISCOURAGING

TOPICS AND IDEAS FOR SELF-REFLECTION AND DISCUSSION

SELF-REFLECTION

"Keep away from people who try to belittle your ambitions. Small people always do that, but the really great make you feel that you, too, can become great." Mark Twain

"Although the world is full of suffering, it is also full of the overcoming of it." Helen Keller

Keep strong.

GROUP DISCUSSION

Discuss the importance of compliments and how compliments can be used to encourage. Discuss the importance of being honest in providing compliments, while encouraging others to follow their dreams.

What are some compliments you can give to friends, family members, and business associates? What kinds of compliments can you give?

CHAPTER 19– REFERENCES AND FURTHER READING

Bradt, G. (July 2, 2019). Compliments and Criticism – Why and How to Encourage More. Available at *https://www. forbes. com/sites/georgebradt/2019/07/02/compliments-and-criticismwhy-and-how-to-encourage-more/?sh=1806569c77d2*

Raghunathan, R. (July 11, 2012). The Art of Complimenting and Criticizing. Psychology Today. Available at *https://www. psychologytoday. com/ca/blog/sapient-nature/201207/the-art-complimenting-and-criticizing*

Suzuki, L. , Davis, H. , & Greenfield, P. (2008). Self-Enhancement and Self-Effacement in Reaction to Praise and Criticism: The Case of Multiethnic Youth. *Ethos, 36*(1), 78-97. Retrieved January 19, 2021.

CHAPTER 20

BUILDING SELF ESTEEM THE 'JOURNAL' WAY

Self-esteem is critical to the development of young people. The better they feel about themselves, the more confidence they develop, and the more able they are to excel in whatever they attempt. The more they excel, the greater their confidence becomes, and the more self-esteem they develop. Therefore, children and young people need to develop self-esteem as early as possible, because it gives them a good start in life.

SELF-ESTEEM OFTEN LACKING

Unfortunately, many young people lack self-esteem, which may hamper their performance in school. However, there are questions about the relationship between self esteem and school performance. While some researchers argue that high self esteem does not lead to good school performance, others argue that high self esteem is partly a result of good school performance (Baumeister, Campbell, Krueger & Vohs, 2003). Poor performance in school has been identified as draining self-esteem in some instances. It then becomes a problem of 'the chicken or the egg'. In many situations, I have seen children and young people who have the ability to perform well, but who are not performing up to mark because they think very little of themselves and of their abilities. They lack the confidence to perform well.

DISPELLING NEGATIVITY

This is not good enough. Although there may be circumstances that may take a toll on a child or young person, every effort should be made to dispel negativity by building positive reinforcements whenever possible, whether at home, at school, or in community organizations. All children must recognize that they are good at something, and that they possess intelligence.

INTELLIGENCE OR INTELLIGENCES?

The definition of intelligence that is commonly used in educational circles has to do with being able to demonstrate linguistic as well as logical and mathematical skills. However, research over the past three or four decades has shown that this definition of intelligence is rather limited and insufficient, considering the new environment in which we live. Today, there are many different sources of information, for example, television, computers, satellites and the Internet, and many more roles for people to play. The new technology is changing our world to one that has to be more inclusive.

DEFINING INTELLIGENCE

A relatively new definition of intelligence, as Harvard professor and researcher, Howard Gardner, noted, is "the ability to produce a product that is valued in a culture or society." In other words, a student who gets an A in a math test should be seen as smart or intelligent, but so should another student who has just played an outstanding piece of music on the piano or steel drum. A student who has just given an outstanding performance in a baseball game, or one who has just created a well-designed garment, should also be recognized as intelligent.

EXCELLENCE NECESSARY FOR INTELLIGENCE

What is critical in this new definition is that intelligence refers to excellence in a product that is valued in society. Although we often think of academics as the most important measure of intelligence and often downplay other activities, if we stop to think we would soon realize that all of these other fields and activities go together to give us a well-rounded life.

ALL ARE VALUABLE FIELDS

Think of what the world would be like if all we had were mathematicians and no musicians! Think of what the world would be like without plumbers. Or if there were no athletes, singers or dancers to entertain! Or no artists to create beauty! Or no engineers to help design our bridges, or no welders to actually join the pieces of metal together to make the bridge! Or no religious leaders to help with our spiritual needs, or no psychiatrists to help us work out our personal issues! All of these fields are valued because of what they add to the human condition.

Gardner, from his research in many countries and cultures, identified seven intelligences. These, he defined, as linguistic, logico-mathematical, spatial, musical, bodily-kinesthetic, interpersonal, and intrapersonal.

LINGUISTIC AND MATHEMATICAL NOT EVERYTHING

Linguistic intelligence covers excellence in reading, writing, speaking and related abilities. Mathematical intelligence refers to excellence in mathematics and in logical thinking. These first two intelligences that Gardner identified cover the skills that the old definition of intelligence covered. These are the skills that are tested when we take an IQ test.

SPATIAL AND MUSICAL

Spatial intelligence refers to excellence in knowing direction, working with maps, seeing relations between things, and being able to draw and do other artistic activities. Musical intelligence involves excellence in music. It could involve having a good ear for music, or being able to sing or play a musical instrument.

BODILY-KINESTHETIC

Bodily-kinesthetic intelligence refers to excellence in controlling one's body, which is evident in individuals who are able to make their bodies perform as they desire. Athletes and dancers have this intelligence, for they are able to achieve the movements they desire. People with this intelligence are aware of their movements in a way that people without this intelligence are unable to do.

INTERPERSONAL

Interpersonal intelligence refers to the great ability some people have for interacting with others, for being able to fit in in any situation, and for feeling comfortable around other people. People with this intelligence could be the "social butterflies" in our networking circles.

INTRAPERSONAL

Intrapersonal intelligence, on the other hand, refers to the ability that some people have in appreciating their own company, being able to be alone and not feel lonely. It also refers to the great sense of confidence and self-esteem that some people have in themselves, regardless of the predicament they may be experiencing.

EXCEL IN SPECIFIC INTELLIGENCE(S)

We excel in some, and usually not in all of these. Some students excel in musical intelligence, some in mathematical, some in interpersonal, and some in spatial. Some students excel in a few or several of these intelligences. Gardner pointed out that traditionally because some of us do not excel in linguistic and mathematical intelligences, we are thought of as not being intelligent. Instead, we should be considered smart in the particular intelligences in which we excel, and should be acknowledged because of this.

DEVELOP YOUR WEAK INTELLIGENCES

As young people, you can therefore take stock of your intelligences and work to improve your performance in the ones in which you are weak. The secret lies in identifying in which intelligences you excel, and in reinforcing them. Equally important is identifying those intelligences in which you are weak. This would help you to focus your attention on improvement. According to Gardner, recognizing your strengths should also alert you to your weaknesses. You should then realize that you have ability, and that your goal should be to reinforce what you have and develop what you lack. A good way to take stock of your intelligences is to keep a journal.

DEVELOP WITH JOURNALS

Researchers have found that the use of journals has helped students of all ages in a variety of ways. Keeping a journal gives the individual an opportunity to express himself or herself freely and regularly. It is like a diary in that it is a place where the individual could write what is on his or her mind. Yet, it is much more than that.

CHAPTER 20 - FOOD FOR THOUGHT – BUILDING SELF ESTEEM THE 'JOURNAL' WAY

TOPICS AND IDEAS FOR SELF-REFLECTION AND DISCUSSION

SELF-REFLECTION

"Self-esteem is made up primarily of two things: feeling lovable and feeling capable." Jack Canfield

Think of the things that you can do well. By creating a journal of all the things you do well, you will be reminding yourself of your competence. Keep seeing yourself as excelling in your areas of competence. In this way you will build confidence. Also, make a list of all the other things that make you feel good about yourself and do them.

"You have been criticizing yourself for years, and it hasn't worked. Try approving of yourself and see what happens. – Louise L. Hay

Don't be so hard on yourself that you are blinded to your accomplishments and your potential!

GROUP DISCUSSION

"Optimism is the faith that leads to achievement. Nothing can be done without hope or confidence."
Helen Keller

Everyone in the group can be encouraged to create a journal.

Discuss what makes people feel good about themselves.

CHAPTER 20 – REFERENCES AND FURTHER READING

Armstrong, T. (2020). Multiple intelligences. American Institute for Learning and Human Development. Available at *https://www. institute4learning. com/resources/articles/multiple-intelligences/*

Baumeister, R. F. , Campbell, J. D. , Krueger, J. J. & Vohs, K. D. (2003). Does high self esteem cause better performance, interpersonal success, happiness, or healthier lifestyles? *Psychological Science in the Public Interest, 4*(1), 1-44.

Gardner, H. (1991). *The Unschooled Mind: How Children Think and How Schools Should Teach.* New York: Basic Books.

Gardner, Howard and T. Hatch (1989). Multiple intelligences go to school: Educational implications of the theory of multiple intelligence. *Educational Researcher, 18*(8), 4-10

CHAPTER 21

HOW TO DEVELOP YOUR INTELLIGENCES WITH JOURNALS

One of the ways to develop your intelligences is through keeping a journal. A journal is a very personal expression, and has been used as a tool for learning. It has also been used as a tool for better self-knowledge and reflection. Several fields, including psychiatry, use this as therapy. On the other hand, journals have been used as a means of sharing ideas in a group. Journals are highly versatile.

SETTING UP YOUR JOURNAL - LINGUISTIC AND MATHEMATICAL AT WORK

You could use a journal to record the areas of your success. You could do this by getting a notebook, and labelling seven sections, each with one of the following headings: Linguistic, Logico-Mathematical, Spatial, Musical, Bodily-kinesthetic, Interpersonal and Intrapersonal. Your linguistic intelligence is being developed as keeping a journal involves writing and reading. Since you have to think about what you will put in your journal, this involves the use of the logico-mathematical intelligence. This intelligence would be further promoted as you have to think of how to organize your journal.

SPATIAL – DRAW AND TAKE PICTURES

Spatial intelligence may also be at work as you may decide that you want to draw, design, or make a special journal. If you go on a trip, take pictures of the various places you visit. You may also want to draw a map on which you locate these places. You may decide to write something about each place that you visit, or give your reflections on your experience of these places, and of the people you meet. You would note this is your intrapersonal intelligence taking over here.

BODILY-KINESTHETIC – PERFORM AND DISPLAY

You may be a good gymnast, athlete, or dancer, or you may enjoy keeping fit. Maybe you play on a basketball team, or maybe you are an outstanding football player. You may include a picture of yourself in one of these roles in the journal, or you may choose to write something about the importance of keeping fit, or why you like the particular activity that you do. This is evidence of your bodily-kinesthetic intelligence at work, but it also draws on your linguistic intelligence.

MUSICAL PRESENTATIONS AND APPRECIATION

You may like music, and may choose to write a song, or you may include a picture of yourself in a band, playing a musical instrument, or rapping. You may also draw a musical instrument, or you may choose to write about the development of a musical instrument, for example, the drums, or you may choose to write a brief history of Carnival or the bagpipes. Maybe you admire a particular musician or singer, or you are very knowledgeable about Rhythm and Blues, Country Music, Hip Hop, Rap, or Classical Music. Regardless of your musical interest and persuasion, you may design your journal to suit. You are putting your musical intelligence to work in this activity.

INTERPERSONAL – INCLUDE YOUR FRIENDS

Maybe you have many friends, or enjoy large family outings. Or maybe you are a good organizer of events. Write about these experiences or include drawings. Maybe you like debates, or you enjoy working with younger children. Maybe you volunteer at an organization and you really enjoy the interaction. Take pictures of your friends and include them in your journal. Maybe you have an all-time special event that you'd never forget. Share your journal with others, if you so choose. All of this is excellent information to support your interpersonal intelligence.

BE REFLECTIVE

Intrapersonal intelligence involves self-reflection, thinking about yourself and being alone. It involves assessing the person that you are and liking yourself for being you. The very act of having created the journal will help develop intrapersonal intelligence, as you think, choose, paint, and design your journal. As you look back at what you have created, you will feel proud of your accomplishment. These are only suggestions, and you could be as creative as you want to be, because it is YOUR journal.

HOW MUCH YOU HAVE TAKEN FOR GRANTED

As you undertake the creation of your journal, you'd realize that there are many accomplishments that you took for granted, or never considered as accomplishments at all. As you create your journal, you'd also notice that there are some areas where you excel, and some areas where you are weak. This is expected. There are very few people who excel in all areas. This exercise, however, gives you something to strive for. As Gardner observes, it should be the goal of everyone to develop all of these intelligences. This exercise of creating your journal would greatly improve your self-esteem, and would be a source of motivation for you to work in new areas. You would be stretching and challenging yourself to be a better YOU.

WHAT ABOUT SOCIAL MEDIA

Many individuals, young and old, use social media to showcase their activities, skills, and lifestyles. While some may consider creating a journal such as this online, the question that must be foremost on their minds is: "Why am I doing this online?" "Is it to show my friends and others how good I am and what good work I can do, or is it for me to identify my different intelligences?" Recognizing their motivations for creating their journals may quickly reveal that a journal such as this is not for showing off what they can do and possibly competing with others, but actually helping them to improve their performance in the different intelligences. Social media may not be a place for a private journal.

CHAPTER 21 - FOOD FOR THOUGHT – HOW TO DEVELOP YOUR INTELLIGENCES

TOPICS AND IDEAS FOR SELF-REFLECTION AND DISCUSSION

SELF-REFLECTION

Consider these two quotes: How do they apply to you?

"Everybody is a genius. But if you judge a fish by its ability to climb a tree, it will live its whole life believing that it is stupid." Albert Einstein

"But once we realize that people had different kinds of minds, different kinds of strengths – some people are good in thinking spatially, some in thinking language, others are very logical, other people need to be hands on and explore actively and try things out-- then education, which treats everybody the same way, is actually the lost unfair education." Howard Gardner

Set up your own journal based on your intelligences.

Think of the many intelligences that you have that you had not thought about before. Think of those intelligences that you can develop and improve.

GROUP DISCUSSION

Take an inventory of the various intelligences you possess as a group and think of the group activities, based on these intelligences, in which you can engage.

Following is an interesting quote from Howard Gardner, the American developmental psychologist, who put forward the theory of multiple intelligences. This could be the subject of group discussion.

"If you are not prepared to resign or be fired for what you believe in, then you are not a worker, let alone a professional. You are a slave." Howard Gardner

CHAPTER 21– REFERENCES AND FURTHER READING

Armstrong, T. (2020). Multiple intelligences. American Institute for Learning and Human Development. Available at *https://www. institute4learning. com/resources/articles/multiple-intelligences/*

Gardner, H. (1994). Creating minds: an anatomy of creativity. *New Scientist, 141*(914).

Gardner, H. (1991). *The Unschooled Mind: How Children Think and How Schools Should Teach.* New York: Basic Books.

Gardner, H. (1983). *Frames of Mind.* New York: Basic Books.

Gardner, Howard and T. Hatch (1989). Multiple intelligences go to school: Educational implications of the theory of multiple intelligence. *Educational Researcher, 18*(8), 4-10.

CHAPTER 22

WHEN PRACTICE IS NECESSARY

It is all too easy to see something done and to conclude that we know how to do it." That's easy!" "I can do that!" "Nothing to it!" That's until we have to actually do it, and then we discover it isn't as easy as we thought it would be. Yet, after we practise the particular activity and get proficient at it, we realize there really is nothing too difficult about it.

AIM FOR PROFICIENCY

We are only truly able to say that we know how to carry out a particular activity when we have practised that activity several times and have developed the skills necessary to do it quickly. Not until we know the sequence of operations and are able to perform them proficiently can we say that we know how to carry out the particular activity.

Take driving, for example. It is a very simple operation to those of us who can drive. However, to acquire the skills involved, we had to learn and practice. Some of us had to take several in-car driving lessons in order to become good enough to pass our driving test. Some of us may have had to take our driving tests twice in order to prove that we had developed the required proficiency. We may have failed our first test, and after failing, we had to practice again until we acquired all the necessary skills.

LOOKS TOO COMPLICATED?

There are other situations in which we decide not to carry out a particular activity because it looks very complicated. Again, the problem is one of practice. If we had taken the time to try out and practise a particular skill, we would have found out that it was quite easy.

COMMON EXPERIENCE

Here is a common experience that many young people have at school. The teacher explains something and works it out on the board. The students see the teacher working out the problem and they tell themselves that they know how to do it. "It's easy!" "I can do that!" Yes, but never having practised the operation independently, the students really cannot say they know how to do the problem completely on their own.

NO PROMPTS IN A TEST

When they are asked to carry out that particular operation, they may know how to start, but may not know what to do next. If they are prompted midway through the problem, they would be able to complete it. But in school, and usually in a test situation, there are usually no prompts from the teacher. Students sometimes end up doing poorly on tests.

PRACTICE BRINGS MASTERY

Now, if the students were to have some practice doing the operations prior to being tested, they would soon have found out what steps came next, and would have remembered the sequence of operations to do the problem. With practice, the students could have mastered the problem and have been successful on their tests.

FAR TOO DIFFICULT

In other instances, students may see a problem worked out on the board and see it as so complicated, that they decide there is no way they could ever do the problem. The students may therefore block their minds, convincing themselves that the problem is far too difficult to understand.

YOU MUST PRACTISE

If students were to have the opportunity to go over the operation, see how the steps followed each other, and then practised these steps, before long they would have become proficient in doing the operation. What is the important lesson here? Remember that practice is the very foundation of learning. If you haven't practised, you really haven't learned!

CHAPTER 22 - FOOD FOR THOUGHT – WHEN PRACTICE IS NECESSARY

TOPICS AND IDEAS FOR SELF-REFLECTION AND DISCUSSION

SELF-REFLECTION

What does practice mean to you?

"Failing to prepare is preparing to fail." **John Wooden**

"Practice does not make perfect, perfect practice makes perfect." Vince Lombardi

GROUP DISCUSSION

"The future belongs to those who prepare for it today." Malcolm X

Discuss ways in which practice can help young people perform better. Read and discuss:*https://ctl. byu. edu/tip/effective-learning-through-practice-skill-building-and-feedback*

CHAPTER 22– REFERENCES AND FURTHER READING

Brabeck, M. , Jeffrey, J. & Fry, S. (2021), Practice for knowledge acquisition (Not drill and kill). American Psychological Association. Available at *https://www. apa. org/education/k12/practice-acquisition*

Center for Teaching and Learning (2021). Effective learning through practice, skill-building, and feedback. Brigham Young University. Available at *https://ctl. byu. edu/tip/effective-learning-through-practice-skill-building-and-feedback*

Hart, J. T. , Jr. (2014). Guided metacognition in instrumental practice. *Music Educators Journal, 101*(2), 57-64

McFarland, E. H. (2014). Facilitating lifelong success: Teaching middle school choristers to practice. *The Choral Journal, 54*(9), 59-64

CHAPTER 23

ARE YOU A GOOD EXAMPLE FOR YOUR YOUNGER SIBLINGS?

Apart from the parent/child relationship, another relationship that is important to a child is that with an older sibling. How often have we seen a young boy imitating his older brother or a young girl trying to be like her older sister!

If you are a young person with a younger sibling, you may recall the first time you discovered you were going to be a big brother or sister. You may have been too young to remember, or maybe you remember not being particularly thrilled with having to give up your special position as the only one. Maybe you were excited about having someone to play with or even to boss around. Maybe you remember the whole older sibling role as evenings of babysitting you'd rather not think about. You may have fought on occasions with your younger sibling or simply threatened him or her for meddling with your things. You may even have followed through on those threats, when your sibling may have read your diary or may have taken stuff out of your room.

THAT'S MY BIG BROTHER

Yet, with the passing years, you must have relished the experience when your younger sibling came to you for help while at school, or may have pointed you out with pride to classmates or friends as "This is my big brother, Reggie," or "That is my big sister, Jackie." You must have felt proud too of the 'little fella' or of your 'cute little sister'.

YOU ARE STILL THE BIG SISTER

But times have changed. You may be fully grown now and things may not be as easy as they once were. You may have gotten mixed up with the wrong crowd, or you may be having a difficult time making the transition to responsibility that comes with approaching adulthood. You may be out of control and believe you are too old to be spoken to, or that your parents have no right to be "on your case". After all, you reason, it is your life, and no one else's business. You may rationalize that if you mess up, you are not hurting anyone, and so people (meaning your parents) should leave you alone and mind their business.

ARE YOU REALLY YOUR OWN PERSON?

Well, you know in your heart that your parents are right, that they care about you and want to see things go right for you. Yet, you are trying to convince yourself that your life should be nobody's business, but yours. You think that you are your own person.

Well, think again. Remember how your baby brother or sister followed you around when you were younger, listened to your every word, and proudly pointed you out as his or her big brother or sister! Remember how your younger sibling imitated you, and thought of you as someone special he or she could trust! Well, not much has changed. Your younger sibling may still be taking his or her cue from you. After all, he or she may still be thinking, "that's my big brother" or 'that's my big sister."

STILL FOLLOWING YOU

Although you may be messing up, that little brother or sister may still be following your example. He or she, although much older now, may be thinking just how brave you are to do the things that you are doing.

ARE YOU A GOOD EXAMPLE?

Think about this. You may be setting a bad example for your younger sibling, who may already be imitating you, and who may already be beginning to do the same things that you are now doing. You may want to rationalize that you never told your younger sibling to follow your example. You didn't have to. He or she has always admired you – always looked up to you.

DO THE RIGHT THING – CLEAN UP YOUR ACT

Therefore, if you are off your course and have a younger brother or sister who may be mirroring your bad example, one of the best things you can do now is to start straightening out your own life. In the meantime, make time to talk to your younger sibling. Let your sibling know that you took the wrong turn, made mistakes and ended up on the wrong side of the tracks. Convince your younger sibling of the dangers of your ways, and encourage him or her to steer the right course before it is too late. Let your younger sibling know how much you regret what you have done, and that you have a sincere desire to make positive changes in your life. If your younger sibling is skipping school or has dropped out, is getting involved with bad company and is being disrespectful to your parents, then you need to help your younger sibling reform his or her ways.

BE THE LEADER YOU WANT TO BE

In doing this, you may find that the relationship with your younger sibling improves and your parents may start taking you a little more seriously, realizing that you really care about your younger brother or sister. So, ask yourself today, "What example am I setting?" and do the right thing.

CHAPTER 23 - FOOD FOR THOUGHT – ARE YOU A GOOD EXAMPLE FOR YOUR YOUNGER SIBLINGS?

TOPICS AND IDEAS FOR SELF-REFLECTION AND DISCUSSION

SELF-REFLECTION

Think about this:

Sometimes, in speaking to their peers, younger siblings often describe their older siblings as perfect beings; and some younger siblings often believe it. But at times, it is important for a sibling to consider that having an older sibling can help him/her learn how to become a good person. This means when your sibling does something good, you can imitate him or her. However, when your sibling does something bad, you can learn what not to do, and realize that no one is perfect.

GROUP DISCUSSION

What are some good examples young people could set for their younger siblings?

In what areas of their lives would providing good examples really pay off huge dividends?

CHAPTER 23– REFERENCES AND FURTHER READING

Davies, K. (2015). Siblings, Stories and the Self: The sociological significance of young people's sibling relationship. *Sociology, 49*(4), 679-695.

Urbatsch, R. (2011). Ideological Influence: A natural experiment. *British Journal of Political Science, 41,* 693-712

CHAPTER 24

FINDING THE LEADER WITHIN YOU

When we think of the term 'leader', we often think in terms of a business executive or the head of a major corporation or political party. These are examples of leaders. However, a leader is really someone who influences and motivates others. One of the definitions that the dictionary gives for the verb 'to lead' is "to guide or direct; to influence, to persuade". The dictionary further defines a 'leader' as 'one who leads'. That means someone who guides, directs, influences or persuades. You can choose to be a good leader.

"ANYONE CAN BE A LEADER"

According to Keith Harrell, a former IBM marketing executive and one of the company's top training instructors, "Anyone can be a leader. You don't have to be in a management position to positively influence others." This includes you. Harrell, who is also a successful leadership coach, maintains: "Everyone should become a leader because it gives us multiple opportunities to pay our rent on this earth by giving back."

MAY SEEM LIKE A CHALLENGE

How can anyone become a leader? This may seem like a challenge to all of us, because leadership is about influencing others, and influencing them for good. However, leadership is also about having a good and positive attitude. Leadership is also about aspiring to be the best that we could be, because that gives us purpose in life. When we know we are fulfilling our important purpose in life, then our life makes sense and this gives us fulfillment and satisfaction.

FULFILLMENT AND SATISFACTION

Fulfillment and satisfaction are therefore the ingredients of a happy life. Despite the fact that many of us aspire to make lots of money, having the material things is not the answer. Money helps us live a comfortable life, but it does not necessarily help us to live a happy and fulfilled life. As Mel Blount, CEO and President of Mel Blount Youth Homes, explains, "Even in the midst of winning NFL championships with the Pittsburgh Steelers, even with the money and the rings, I knew it wasn't the material things that mattered. What mattered was whether I was at peace with myself. What mattered was whether I was proud of who I was. What mattered was whether I had a sense of purpose" (Mel Blount, quoted in Harrell, 2003).

FULFILLING YOUR PURPOSE

Having a purpose, to be the best that you can be and to influence others positively, puts you on the road to becoming a great leader. Being a leader also means being honest, possessing integrity, being dedicated, having a sense of accountability, and inspiring others to follow a similar pattern in becoming a good leader.

BE HONEST

We have to be honest in what we say and do, so others, knowing that we will not deceive them, can take us at our word. We must have integrity, be the person who keeps his or her word, and who lives by certain good principles. We must be dedicated. We must demonstrate that we can believe in something worthwhile, that we can aspire to be someone special and dedicated to a good cause. Just as important is accountability. We must be accountable for our actions, and for whatever we undertake. This means that we should be thorough and take an interest in whatever we are engaged in, realizing that we should be able at all times to give good account of our behavior or what is in our care. By living by these principles of leadership, we influence others to be good leaders as well.

"LEADERSHIP IS CONTAGIOUS"

As an effective leader and adhering to these principles, you can't help but influence others positively, for as Harrell points out: "Leadership is contagious, in the best sense of the word. A commitment to be our best and to inspire others to be their best sets up a leadership legacy that motivates others to respond in kind" (Harrell, 2003).

REALIZE YOUR POTENTIAL FOR GOOD

Therefore, as a young person, realize your potential for good. By having a good and positive attitude, by having a purpose in life, and by aspiring to be your best, you will be influencing others, particularly your peers, to do the same thing. Think of being the good and effective leader you can be by influencing others through your honesty, your integrity, your dedication, and your accountability. By setting the bar high, you will see that leadership is truly contagious and that others would see you as an example to emulate.

CHAPTER 24 - FOOD FOR THOUGHT – FINDING THE LEADER WITHIN YOU

TOPICS AND IDEAS FOR SELF-REFLECTION AND DISCUSSION

SELF-REFLECTION

"Be more concerned with your character than your reputation, because your character is what you really are, while your reputation is merely what others think you are." John Wooden

"Try not to become a man of success but rather try to become a man of value." Albert Einstein

GROUP DISCUSSION

Discuss with your group what you believe an ideal leader is.

How can you distinguish between a good leader and a bad leader?

What are some of the distinguishing features to look for?

Can a bad leader make changes to become a good leader? Is this possible? If it is, what are some of the changes that would have to be undertaken to make this transformation work?

CHAPTER 24 – REFERENCES AND FURTHER READING

Bar, R. J. & DeSouza, J. F. X. (2016). Tracking Plasticity: Effects of Long-Term Rehearsal in Expert Dancers Encoding Music to Movement. *PLOS ONE*, 2016; 11 (1): e0147731 *DOI: 10. 1371/journal. pone. 0147731*

Ellman, M (May 21, 2019). Practice makes Better! but only if…World of Better Learning. Cambridge Organization. Available at *https://www. cambridge. org/elt/blog/2019/05/21/practice-makes-perfect/*

Harrell, K. (2003). *The Attitude of Leadership: Taking the Lead and Keeping It.* New Jersey and Toronto: John Wiley & Sons, Inc.

Tomines, J. (2020). Practice makes Better. EdTechTeam. Available at *https://www. edtechteam. com/blog/2017/10/practice-makes-better/*

CHAPTER 25

DEVELOPING YOUR LEADERSHIP ABILITIES

Honesty, integrity, dedication and accountability are very important elements in leadership. However, as John C. Maxwell, a leadership guru, explains, there are many other facets of leadership, including "respect, experience, emotional strength, people skills, discipline, vision, momentum (and) timing." All of these elements and facets do not spring up overnight; they develop over time. Therefore, it is necessary to understand the Law of Process (Maxwell, 2002). This simply means that to become a good and effective leader, you need to start cultivating the qualities that will bring this about. What better time than NOW! And these are qualities that you would continue developing for the rest of your life: you become better as you work on them.

WORKING TOWARDS REALIZATION OF A WORTHY IDEAL

You may be asking: "Why should I aspire to be a leader? All I want is to make a success of my life, and that's it." The interesting thing about leadership is that you need it to be the greatest success possible in whatever you undertake. And what is success? It's working towards the realization of a worthy ideal, regardless of what that ideal is (Napoleon Hill and Clement Stone, 2010). Without leadership, you would not be all that you can be.

THE LAW OF THE LID

As John Maxwell explains, there is another important theory we must consider: "the Law of the Lid." "Leadership ability is the lid that determines a person's level of effectiveness. The lower an individual's ability to lead, the lower the lid on his (her) potential." If you do not raise the level of the lid, in other words, if you do not improve your leadership abilities, you will be putting a limit on your own growth and achievement.

NOTABLE EXAMPLE OF LEADERSHIP

To illustrate the significance of leadership in reaching individual potential, Maxwell tells the story of two brothers, Dick and Maurice, who in 1937 started selling hotdogs, fries and shakes in the parking lot of their small restaurant to customers who wanted to eat in their cars. The brothers used carhops to take orders and deliver meals to their customers, whom they served on good china dishes. The brothers made $50,000 in profits a year.

In 1940, the brothers changed locations, added more items on the menu, including barbecued beef, pork sandwiches and hamburgers, and substituted paper products for the china. In 1948, they got rid of the carhops, reduced their menu to mainly hamburgers, and allowed customers to walk in and order their meals. They also shortened the length of time it took to serve their customers. The brothers doubled their profits to $100,000. These brothers demonstrated that they were high on creative ideas and hard work, and so they succeeded in making their restaurant a success.

LOW ON LEADERSHIP – LOST OUT ON FORTUNE

However, they were low on an important ingredient: leadership. The level of their lid was low. In 1954, Ray Kroc, who was high on leadership abilities, or whose lid had a high level, approached the McDonald brothers, Dick and Maurice, and bought the first franchise of the McDonald's restaurant. Kroc worked hard, learning the business, and in 1961, he bought the exclusive rights to McDonald's from the two brothers. When Kroc offered the brothers the sum of $2. 7 million, they must have considered it a great fortune at the time!

With Kroc's leadership, the small restaurant multiplied into thousands of franchised restaurants, and today McDonald's dominates the fast-food industry in many countries. Kroc's leadership, combined with the hard work and creativity of the McDonald's brothers, brought this to fruition. Imagine if the McDonald's brothers had the leadership abilities to combine with their hard work and creativity. They would have netted the $2. 7 million for which they sold their small restaurant thousands of times over!

HAVING ALL THE RIGHT INGREDIENTS

This analogy could apply to many situations. By having good people skills, by cultivating discipline, by displaying vision, by having momentum and by recognizing good timing, Ray Kroc was able to see an opportunity and develop it, not only for himself, but for the thousands of people who bought his franchise. Besides, he was also respectful of the MacDonald brothers and of their ideas. Kroc took time to gain experience, and showed the emotional strength necessary to develop these ideas into something phenomenal. He raised the lid and the level of his effectiveness. If you adopt the Law of the Lid and develop your leadership abilities, you will find you will be more effective in whatever you undertake. Leadership is therefore for everyone; not just for the heads of corporations.

But leadership is about much more than this. To be a leader entails having character traits, skills, emotional intelligence and other characteristics that cause people to be drawn to such a person and to look up to that person for direction. More than that, being a good leader involves not being a bully, but being someone who respects others and who possesses the characteristics of honesty, integrity, dedication and accountability. Being a leader also involves having a vision and the discipline to pursue that vision.

CHAPTER 25 - FOOD FOR THOUGHT – DEVELOPING YOUR LEADERSHIP ABILITIES

TOPICS AND IDEAS FOR SELF-REFLECTION AND DISCUSSION

SELF-REFLECTION

"You cannot teach a man anything; you can only help him find it within himself." **Galileo Galilei**

"The greatest leader is not necessarily the one who does the greatest things. He is the one that gets the people to do the greatest things." - Ronald Reagan

GROUP DISCUSSION

What do you think leadership abilities are? Consider this quote for ideas.

"Average leaders raise the bar on themselves; good leaders raise the bar for others; great leaders inspire others to raise their own bar." - Orrin Woodward

CHAPTER 25– REFERENCES AND FURTHER READING

Harrell, K. (2003). *The Attitude of Leadership: Taking the Lead and Keeping It.* New Jersey and Toronto: John Wiley & Sons, Inc.

Hill, N. & Stone, C. (2010). *Success through a positive mental attitude.* Ishi Press

Maxwell, J. C. (2002*). Leadership 101: What Every Leader Needs to Know.* Tennessee: Thomas Nelson, Inc.

Maxwell, J. C. (1999). *The Indispensable Qualities of a Leader: Becoming the Person Others Will Want to Follow.* Tennessee: Thomas Nelson, Inc.

CHAPTER 26

STUDENT LEADERSHIP FOR IMPROVED EDUCATION?

We live in a society that believes in assigning blame. Think of practically any situation – at home, at school, at work, in government, anywhere. When something goes wrong, our first concern is often not with "what went wrong and how to fix it," but rather, with "Whose fault is it?" We become so preoccupied with pointing out the individual or group that was not doing his, her, or its job, that in many cases the problem remains unfixed for considerable periods. While this approach may seem appropriate for many, as they shift responsibility to others, it usually doesn't serve anyone's good.

This is an even more serious concern when we think of our education system. While a large number of young people are doing well in school, many of them excelling, there are many others that are failing miserably.

ASSIGNING BLAME-"WHOSE FAULT IS IT?"

The general approach we take is one of assigning blame. This "blame approach" is also a "deficit" approach, because it focuses on highlighting those individuals and institutions that were deficit in what they were supposed to do. We blame parents for being deficit in their responsibility to their children. "They didn't make sure their children did their homework", or simply, "They are lousy parents." We blame the teacher for the child's failure. "The teacher just doesn't care enough about the student to make sure that the student learns." We blame the school administrators for not implementing the right programs or policies, and for depending on textbook publishers to determine the appropriate curriculum for classroom use. We blame the unions and teachers' organizations for being more concerned with the teachers and not showing enough concern for parents and students. Parents, government, teachers, boards, unions and teachers' organizations, all hurl accusations at each other with respect to the functioning of the education system. There is enough blame to go around, for we could blame a host of other individuals and institutions for the fact that some students are failing miserably in the education system. Each individual or group blames the other, feeling justified in assigning blame, while the other individual or group tries to minimize responsibility.

"IS IT THE STUDENTS' FAULT?"

What happens in the meantime? As individuals and groups blame each other for the state of the education system, the students who are doing poorly and who are failing continue to perform at the same dismal level. Many go through school, coming out functionally illiterate.

If all of these individuals and groups were to gather in an effort to do something about the problem, we would succeed in doing something meaningful. But many efforts at finding the answer fail. We fail because we take the deficit approach. Discussions become mired down in stalemates, because these discussions do not move beyond the point of assigning blame.

TAKE A COMPETENCE APPROACH

We are all guilty of this. We could make a change by taking a 'competence' approach. Some students are failing, although all concerned want to see success. A competence approach would look at things differently.

PARENTS WANT THEIR CHILDREN'S SUCCESS

Using the competence lens to view the fact that there are large numbers of students in the education system that are failing, we would see parents as wanting their children's success in school, and wanting to be competent parents. The focus would then be on making sure that parents know what to do to help their children to be successful.

TEACHERS WANT THEIR STUDENTS' SUCCESS

We must acknowledge that teachers also want to see their students succeed. Teachers strive for competence in the way they go about their work, but again, as in the case of parents, teachers may be competent, and want to know how to motivate particular students to achieve, and what resources they should use to achieve these goals. Many teachers know what resources and facilities they need to promote learning and want to be better equipped to help students learn.

STUDENTS WANT TO SUCCEED

Students want to be successful, too, although they may try to mask their failure by displaying disdain for school, by cutting classes, and by being rude to their teachers. The competence approach tells us that students would be good students if they knew how to be. These students want to know what they have to do to succeed.

SCHOOL ADMINISTRATORS WANT TO SUCCEED

School administrators may be competent administrators and want to know what programs to implement that would meet the needs of particular students.

Governments want to be thought of as competent leaders, and want to demonstrate their competence in the decisions they make. They may be so convinced of the rightness of their own methods that they do not look at what other stakeholders are saying. They do not take the time to realize that market approaches to education may need to be changed. What is lacking in all of this is a focused look on areas of need that should be addressed, without faulting or blaming any one group.

MAYBE THEY ARE NOT LISTENING
TO EACH OTHER

Maybe groups are not listening to each other, because they are too busy blaming each other for the problem of poor student performance. What seems to be happening is that each group believes that its position is right, without giving sufficient attention to what other groups are saying. This is a very complicated situation, and one that needs each group to listen and make compromises that would put students first. While this may not be something that could be fixed all at once, willingness on the part of all groups to listen and work together to put high priority on a common goal, student success for all, would be a good first step.

In the meantime, there are failing students who may be so convinced that all these other stakeholders are to be blamed, that they see no reason to try and take responsibility for learning. A vicious circle ensues, with students looking at all the things that interfere with their success.

MAKING SCHOOL LESS STRESSFUL

However, efforts are being taken in some areas to deal with the issue of improving education for young people. One of these approaches call for students identifying the reasons for their poor performance. Studies based on poor student performance focus on surveying students in an effort to have them identify their problems (Pope, Brown & Miles, 2015; Villeneuve, Conner, Selby & Pope, 2019).

Surveys reveal that in some schools students experience a great deal of stress, the top sources of stress for high school students being school work, prospect of getting into college after high school, and the financial state of their families (American Psychological Association, 2014, in Villeneuve et al, 2019). A survey carried out in a school where some students were not performing well revealed that some of these students were not getting an adequate number of hours of sleep per night, that some were stressed out over school work, particularly "grades, quizzes, tests, exams, and other assessments" as well as extracurricular activities, and many had little confidence in their ability to cope with these stressors (Villeneuve et al. , 2019).

STUDENT SUGGESTIONS TO EASE STRESS

When students were asked what would help them cope with some of their stressors and improve their performance, they provided several suggestions. For example, some wanted more opportunities for interaction between students and teachers; more academic support from their teachers; and coordination among teachers with respect to the workload so that projects and other work were not all due at the same time (Pope et al., 2015). Other suggestions included reduction in amount of homework given or even elimination of homework on weekends and during breaks; having more time to do homework in school; and having school start at a later time (Pope et al., 2015).

While some of these suggestions may appear reasonable to alleviate the stress that some students experience because of school work, the issues related to homework may be seen as impractical. From experience working with students, most teachers would say that homework is necessary to reinforce what is taught in the class. (I found that students who did their homework consistently usually did better in class than those who often skipped their homework). However, too much homework could become burdensome to both students and to their parents who want to help.

Therefore, one of the ways that students could be helped to perform better would see parents, teachers and students all working together to make school a less stressful place for students. Students must take leadership in speaking up about the problems that they face.

GIVING MORE VOICE TO STUDENTS

Many students do not thrive in the school system because they do not see themselves represented in the classroom or because they do not have a voice to say what is not working for them. Changes are needed and students must be able to point out what is not working. However, schools are based on rules and students are required to follow the rules and learn in a standardized way. But students are unique individuals who do not all learn the same way. When school systems expect all students to learn alike, they do a disservice to those students who do not learn in the expected ways. These students are often thought of as not being able to meet the challenge and follow the rules, and so are often seen as failures.

However, in recent years, educators are becoming more aware of the fact that students learn differently and so are more inclined to adapt their teaching styles to accommodate these different learning styles.

PROMOTING STUDENT VOICE AND LEADERSHIP

But apart from learning styles, students differ based on their life experiences and cultural backgrounds, and this is expected with many different cultural groups making up society. Some schools promote the idea of making 'safe space' for students to express themselves, where students could speak up and participate. But even within this 'safe space', some students do not feel comfortable, and may think that they are not resilient enough to fit into their teachers' expectations.

'SAFE SPACE' AND MARGINALIZED STUDENTS

These students who may not feel comfortable often come from "racialized, marginalized, and underserved populations" (RSEKN, 2019) and may not feel that they can truly express how they feel. Teachers and other adults usually believe that they have created safe space for all, but what they have really done is to create a space that is static and one that fits their expectations. Some teachers and other adults believe that what is safe for them must be safe for all their students (RSEKN, 2019). They insist on certain rules being followed and allow little or no opportunity for deviation.

WHEN LEARNING IS MEANINGFUL

Many students who do not feel safe to express themselves do not find their classrooms culturally meaningful for them. The documentary, This is Not A Resilience Story, gives examples of "how educators might address, challenge, promote, and support issues related to equity, inclusion, and student voice in their respective schools, boards, communities, and beyond" (RSEKN, 2019). Educators are encouraged to think of ways of engaging student voice, affirming what these students have to say, and treating them in 'non –tokenizing' ways (RSEKN, 2019). This recommended approach frees these students who may not be performing well to feel safe within their classrooms to express themselves and to fully participate in the creation of knowledge.

FREEDOM TO DEVIATE FROM RIGID RULES

One result of this approach would be to free these students to deviate from the rules and standardization and to enable them to become part of a community where they could explore different kinds of knowledge that are meaningful to them. Students learn when they see what they are learning is meaningful to them. As Curtis (2019) explains, "According to Self-Determination Theory (SDT), one possible reason for ... disengagement (of marginalized students) is that these students do not perceive their psychological needs for autonomy, belonging and competence as met, which may lead to reduced motivation, and therefore reduced engagement." If students do not see the classroom as meaningful to them, they will not be motivated to perform well. If students do not feel 'valued' and 'safe' in the classroom, they will not feel a sense of belonging (White, October 9, 2019).

ALL STAKEHOLDERS MUST WORK TOGETHER

From the research as well as from my experience, I believe that it's no time for casting blame on parents, teachers, administrators, students, and other stakeholders in the education system. Recognizing that a better understanding is needed, these stakeholders must work together to improve the quality of education and the performance of all students. Students must be encouraged to speak up and the classroom should be an environment where all students feel safe to express themselves and to be respected for their ideas. Students must be able to take leadership in expressing their ideas, and teachers must strive to create meaningful environments and experiences where all their students can succeed. Parents are to be supportive of their children and their children's teachers. Students must recognize that they must take responsibility for their learning, and parents and teachers must be reasonable in the demands they make on their children and students. Administrators must support teachers as teachers strive to meet their curricular requirements while at the same time creating instructional materials that are relevant and meaningful for all their students. Governments, education departments, unions, and all those who provide the environment in which schools operate, must think in terms of providing resources and not depending solely on the market system to determine how the needs of students are met. The education of all our students must be top priority.

CHAPTER 26 - FOOD FOR THOUGHT – STUDENT LEADERSHIP FOR IMPROVED EDUCATION? TOPICS AND IDEAS FOR SELF-REFLECTION AND DISCUSSION

SELF-REFLECTION

What stressors do you see students and young people experiencing?

What are your stressors around school, work, etc. ?

"Trying to be a perfectionist brings increased stress and hinders performance" Theodore Whitmore

GROUP DISCUSSION

What stressors do you see students, teachers, and administrators having around school and improved performance for students?In your group setting, discuss some of the realistic measures that could be undertaken that would lead to less stress on the part of all stakeholders, and that would accomplish the common goal of better school performance and outcome.

CHAPTER 26 – REFERENCES AND FURTHER READING

American Psychological Association (2014). *Stress in America: Are teens adopting adults' stress habits.* Washington, D. C.

Christenson, Sandra L. (2004). The family-school partnership: An opportunity to promote the learning competence of all students. *School Psychological Review, 33*(1).

Curtis, N. L. (2019). Seeking alternative pathways: an exploration of school engagement from the perspectives of marginalized youth. Available at *https://open. library. ubc. ca/cIRcle/collections/ubctheses/24/items/1. 0379313*

Gehl, N. (2020). How to better support your marginalized students. The Art of education. Available at *https://theartofeducation. edu/2019/09/02/how-to-better-support-your-marginalized-students/*

Lawrence, E. C. & Heller, M. B. (2002). Parent-school collaboration: the utility of a competence lens. *Canadian Journal of School Psychology, 17*(1), 5-15.

Pope, D. C. , Brown, M. , & Miles, S. (2015). *Overloaded and Underprepared: Strategies for stronger schools and healthy, successful kids.* San Francisco: Jossey-Bass.

Réseau de Savoir sur l'Équité/ Equity Knowledge Network (RSEKN) (2019). This is not a Resilience Story - Documentary on Child & Youth Voice. Available at *https://youthrex. com/video/this-is-not-a-resilience-story-documentary-on-child-youth-voice*

Villeneuve, J. C. , Conner, J. O. , Selby, S. , Pope, D. C. (2019). Easing the stress at pressure-cooker schools. *The Phi Delta Kappan, 101*(3), 15-19.

White, S. V. (October 9, 2019). Creating a learning environment where all kids feel valued. George Lucas Educational Foundation. Available at https://open. library. ubc. ca/cIRcle/collections/ubctheses/24/items/1. 0379313

CHAPTER 27

DEMONSTRATING GOOD CITIZENSHIP

Demonstrating good citizenship involves behaving in a manner that can be described as law-abiding, humanitarian, respectful of difference, appreciative of diversity, desirous of social justice, and respectful of life. It also involves loving and valuing peace, and recognizing the potential that lies in believing in the power of peace. Good citizenship also recognizes the importance of speaking out against injustice and practicing non-violence.

As Mahatma Gandhi, the Indian lawyer, politician and social activist, who promoted non-violence, noted, "A small body of determined spirits fired by an unquenchable faith in their mission can alter the course of history." Closer home was Martin Luther King, Jr., Baptist minister, civil rights leader, and Nobel Prize winner for peace, who explained, "Peace is not merely a distant goal that we seek but means by which we arrive at that goal." Dr. King advocated standing up for justice as being an example of good citizenship, for as he further noted, "Commit yourself to the noble struggle for equal rights. You will make a greater person of yourself, a greater nation of your country, and a finer world to live in." Through promoting peace, a good citizen could play his or her part in changing the course of history.

What does it mean to be a citizen? It means recognizing that there are rights for citizens, but that these rights also come with responsibilities

RESPONSIBILITIES OF CITIZENSHIP

These include the responsibility to obey your country's laws, the responsibility to vote in elections, the responsibility to respect each other's rights, the responsibility to respect public places, such as parks, schools, and museums, as well as private homes and businesses, and the responsibility to actively care for the environment. Demonstrating good citizenship therefore involves respecting and obeying the law, respecting other people, promoting peace and abhorring violence, striving for fairness and equity, and recognizing all the responsibilities of citizenship. This includes living in harmony with other people groups, not engaging in name-calling, not engaging in violence, not belonging to gangs, and respecting each other's cultural differences.

BASIC REQUIREMENTS FOR CITIZENSHIP

Citizenship also requires becoming knowledgeable about one's government, and when old enough, taking part in electing those who demonstrate they are worthy of holding political office. It even involves members of a society making decisions to run for office, if they believe they have something to contribute, if they see service as most practical in their contribution, and if they are dedicated to putting country above personal interests.

But citizenship is also about caring for others in our society. We are our brothers' keepers and this requires all citizens, whether young or old, to think about those who may be disadvantaged or who may be having a difficult time in life. It becomes our responsibility as citizens to ensure that our resources are so well distributed that no one suffers because of lack of basic needs. We, as citizens, are required to give as much of our time as possible volunteering and giving what we can to help others. Sometimes, the greatest need is for time, time to spend with someone who may be alone.

CHAPTER 27 - FOOD FOR THOUGHT – DEMONSTRATING GOOD CITIZENSHIP

TOPICS AND IDEAS FOR SELF-REFLECTION AND DISCUSSION

SELF-REFLECTION

"Citizenship is the chance to make a difference to the place where you belong." Charles Handy

"We can never get a re-creation of community and heal our society without giving our citizens a sense of belonging." 'Patch' Adams

What do you think the rights and responsibilities of citizenship are?

GROUP DISCUSSION

One of the ways of being a good citizen is ensuring the wellbeing of the society. Discuss this following quote by one of America's leading civil rights leader.

"If you see something that is not right, not fair, not just, you have a moral obligation to say something about it." John Lewis.

John Lewis was a democratic congressman for the United States House of Representatives for Georgia's 5th congressional district from 1987-2020. He was also a civil rights activist and leader who strove very hard for promoting equal rights for Blacks and other groups in his country. Lewis died on July 17.

As a group activity, complete a poster on John Lewis's life and his accomplishments, including the significance of the Edmund Pettus Bridge.

Being a good citizen also involves volunteering and helping those who may be disadvantaged. A former Secretary-General of the United Nations and 2001 Nobel Peace Prize winner gave us this advice:

"Let us remember the large numbers of citizens who, day in and day out, through acts of volunteerism large and small, bring hope to so many of the

world's disadvantaged. Let us ensure that this wonderful resource, available in abundance to every nation, is recognized and supported as it works towards a more prosperous and peaceful world."
Kofi Annan

CHAPTER 27– REFERENCES AND FURTHER READING

American Government (2008-2020). Democratic values – Liberty, equality, Justice. Available at *https://www. ushistory. org/gov/1d. asp*

Bryant, Jr. , J. A. (November-December 2006). What is good citizenship? The story of Chiune Sugihara. Available at *https://www. socialstudies. org/system/files/publications/articles/yl 190213. pdf*

Thorson, K. (October 3, 2012). What does it mean to be a good citizen? Citizenship vocabularies as resources for action. *The Annals of American Academy of Political and Social Science, 644(1), 70-85.*

CHAPTER 28

VOTING IS SPEAKING

Many adults argue that it doesn't really matter how or even if they vote, because the outcome would be the same: "six in one, half a dozen in the other." This is usually held with respect to having candidates from different parties who are very close on the same issues. The argument is that it doesn't matter which candidate gets elected. Some people are influenced by polls and when the candidate they want to win seems to be doing poorly, according to the polls, they may decide that their vote may not matter. In some instances, some people may decide that their candidate is already winning, and so it doesn't matter whether they vote or not. In either of these cases, such thinking can be detrimental to the particular candidate that they support.

EVERY VOTE MATTERS

Just imagine, five thousand people thinking the same way these adults do, and it is not impossible! It is enough to turn the tide of an election, and cause their favorite candidate to lose!!Under these circumstances, every vote matters. If people don't vote, they really aren't taking part in the electoral process. They aren't doing their civic duty, and worst of all, they are denying themselves a voice.

Maybe you are still too young to vote, but you are not too young to prepare yourself. In order to make the right decisions about the direction your country should take, you need to know what is going on. You need to learn how government works, to know that there are different levels of government, national/federal, state/provincial and municipal, and to understand the responsibilities that each of these different levels must carry out. But you need to know more about where political parties stand, and even more importantly, to know where candidates stand on important issues. After all, when you vote, you are electing representatives to speak on your behalf.

BECOME INFORMED

As a young person, you need to become informed about important issues facing your country now, for in a matter of years, you would be one of the people making decisions through your vote as to what should happen. Or better yet, you may be one of the candidates running for office. Without adequate information and preparation, you would not know the issues and the history of the issues, and would not know what position will best serve the people. You would be ill-prepared for either of these roles. Remember, you are supposed to be a thinking person. This means that you should be informed enough not to get caught up in a tide of rhetoric-based inaccuracies and innuendos, that would lead you to accept misinformation as truth.

A VOTER NEEDS RELIABLE INFORMATION

As a voter, you need to have reliable information. Trying to vote without knowledge would be a travesty, since you would be either misusing, or not using, the most powerful instrument you have in our democracy: your vote. When you know what the issues are, when you know where the political parties stand, then you cannot be tricked into supporting a candidate who just does not represent your interests. Knowing the various positions, taking a stand, discussing it with your family members, and having meaningful discussions with your friends would help you understand issues better.

But most importantly, despite what you are told, use your own mind to reason among alternatives given, and make decisions based not on hope or wishes, but rather on reality.

TAKE CONTROL OF THE INFORMATION YOU USE

Unfortunately, many of us are influenced by organizations that have their own interests at heart. In many instances, the interests of the common people may not be reflected in the positions organizations take. Since we sometimes allow people in authority to tell us what to think and what to do, we end up supporting positions that run counter to our own interests. Unfortunately, in many instances, when all is told, it is too late.

Therefore, let us not depend on others to do our thinking for us. It is also in our interests to do our due diligence and fact-check what we hear. It is good to have a certain amount of skepticism and check things out for ourselves. This does not mean being swayed by the crowd, since in many cases, the crowd simply follows what is popular. But remember, what is popular is often not right.

Let us decide for ourselves when something is right. Let us not allow anyone or charismatic figures to convince us that what they are saying is truth, when our gut, our reasoning, and our commonsense tell us it is not. Let's be careful with how we exercise the most important thing we have as individuals: our voice. Let us make our voices heard when we vote. When we don't vote, we let the voices of others be heard, and we lose our opportunity to have a say. We betray those who have gone before us and who have made sacrifices, so that we have the right to vote.

CHAPTER 28 - FOOD FOR THOUGHT – VOTING IS SPEAKING

TOPICS AND IDEAS FOR SELF-REFLECTION AND DISCUSSION

SELF-REFLECTION

(Think:Why should I vote?)

"The vote is precious. It is the most powerful non-violent tool we have in a democratic society, and we must use it." John Lewis

GROUP DISCUSSION

Discuss the meanings of these two quotes.

"Our lives begin to end the day we become silent about things that matter." Dr. Martin Luther King, Jr. , a Baptist Minister, and leader of the Civil Rights movement in the United States from 1955 to 1968 when he was assassinated

"Bad officials are elected by good citizens who do not vote." George Jean Nathan

CHAPTER 28– REFERENCES AND FURTHER READING

Castleton University (October 27, 2020). The Importance of voting. Available at *https://www. castleton. edu/news-media/article/the-importance-of-voting/*

National Geographic (May 11, 2020). Why voting is important. Resource Library. Available at *https://www. nationalgeographic. org/article/why-voting-important/*

Vincentian Partnership for Social Justice (2021). Why Vote. Available at *https://www. vote. ie/why/*

CHAPTER 29

LEADERSHIP IN PERSPECTIVE

WHAT IS LEADERSHIP

Leadership is usually discussed within the context of business corporations and organizations, and a leader is often thought of as a person leading an organization or being a boss in a corporation. But leadership is also a concept that is relevant to all areas of life and endeavors and extends far "beyond the job", with a leader being someone who has influence on others.

Leadership is also a field of study in its own right. This chapter does not claim to provide a comprehensive study of this concept, because such a study is outside the scope of this work. However, to put the discussion of "leadership beyond the job" into focus, this chapter will give some insight into how leadership is formally thought about and how leadership can be perceived on a more personal level.

NO ONE THEORY OR APPROACH APPLIES

There are several leadership theories and different classifications of theories that are mostly used in explaining how leaders behave. Some of these formal theories of leadership reveal that when faced with leading, many individuals use a variety of ideas. This is because in leadership, there are many common attributes that must be present if a leader is to be judged effective in his or her particular circumstance.

In explaining how "leadership beyond the job" is expressed and realized, this paper looked at some common attributes identified as essential leadership characteristics and which are also essential if everyday individuals are to live successful and effective lives outside of a job setting. While some descriptions of leadership are based on theories that are formally constructed, some are also based on Traits leadership theory, with varied characteristics, attitudes, behaviors, abilities, skills, knowledge, and expertise used to describe effective leadership.

CLASSIFICATION OF LEADERSHIP THEORIES

A short overview of leadership theories are in place to show what is happening in the field of leadership today. According to some thinkers, there are four theories of leadership, namely, traits theory, contingency theory, behavioral theory and full-range models of leadership (Jewett-Geragosian, 2018). This classification of leadership theories is broad. The first of the four theories is Traits theory, which identifies the characteristics or qualities that effective leaders should have. The contingency theory of leadership holds that there are some traits that are observed among effective leaders, but that while some traits are effective in some situations, they are not in others. In other words, this theory shows that there is "no single psychological profile or set of enduring links directly to effective leadership" primarily because it is the interrelationship between the individual leader and the existing conditions that determines what is effective (Jewett-Geragosian, 2018). The behavioral theory of leadership looks at leadership as a set of behaviors, based on reward and punishment and the degree to which these cause the modification of a leader's behavior. The full-range theory of leadership is based on the idea that motivation and morale are based on the employee's sense of identity to a project and the collective identity of the organization (Jewett-Geragosian, 2018).

TWO MOST COMMON THEORIES OF LEADERSHIP

The two most common theories of leadership are transactional and transformational. These are part of the full-range theory of leadership. Over the years, several theories of leadership have been forwarded.

TRANSACTIONAL AND TRANSFORMATIONAL LEADERSHIP

Transactional leadership is leadership based on an agreement between a leader and followers with respect to performance goals, where the leader provides incentives to the followers to achieve specified goals and where followers agree to perform as required for compensation or award. Transformational leadership theory, on the other hand, holds that leaders motivate and inspire their followers, and provide a vision around which followers could gravitate. Transformational leaders provide mentoring and coaching to followers, while at the same time enabling followers to take ownership of their work. More than that, transformational leaders provide an ethical environment and are concerned about the interests of their followers, while followers are able to develop an organizational culture where they work for organizational good. Leaders and followers are on the same page. Transformational leaders put emphasis on being authentic, cooperative, and empathic in dealing with their followers, and consider their followers' sense of worth. However, there are other theories of leadership that should be noted.

OTHER COMMON THEORIES OF LEADERSHIP

Other leadership theories that have garnered much attention are also described in terms of styles of leadership. Some of these are autocratic/authoritarian, democratic, participative/democratic, laissez-faire, bureaucratic, situational, servant and charismatic (Arenas et al. , 2017; Kuhnert & Lewis, 1987; Rowold, 2014). Autocratic/authoritarian style of leadership sees the leader retaining as much power and decision making as possible, while democratic leadership sees followers as encouraged to participate in decision making. Laissez-faire leadership is a form of leadership where the leader takes a hands-off approach and puts responsibility for leadership in the hands of the followers. Some think of this type of leadership as an actual abdication of leadership. A bureaucratic style of leadership is where leaders manage by the book, and where everything is done according to procedure (Khan, Khan, Qureshi, Ismail, Rauf et al. , 2015). Situational leadership is where the leader is prepared to change strategy depending on changing situations. Servant leadership is based on the commitment of the leader to serve (Eva, Robin, Sendjaya, van Dierendonck, & Liden, 2019), while charismatic leadership is based on the leader being more of a visionary, able to attract a very committed following because of the trust placed in him or her (House & Howell, 1992; Colbert, Judge, Choi & Wang, 2012). But then there are several other theories of leadership, which are variants of the more dominant theories.

However, a theory that seems to be relevant in defining effective leaders is Traits Theory of Leadership and this is often discussed in the self-help and positive psychology genres.

TRAITS THEORY OF LEADERSHIP

Traits theory is also a common theory that identifies certain personal characteristics that play an important part in the effectiveness of a leader. According to one study, the traits that are considered important "include dimensions of personality and motives, sets of skills and capabilities and behaviors in social relations" (Jewett-Geragosian, 2018). Some of the personality patterns such as adaptability; traits such as task competence, intelligence, conscientiousness, openness to experience, and emotional stability; and interpersonal attributes, such as extroversion and agreeableness, turn out to be important for effective leadership.

WHAT IS GOOD AND EFFECTIVE LEADERSHIP

However, in the search for good leadership, many scholars stress characteristics that are found in those leaders that are considered effective. What seem to stand out most when looking at effective leaders are their traits, abilities, skills, attitudes, qualities, behaviors, knowledge and expertise. In short, good leaders are identified by certain characteristics that they possess.

CHARACTERISTICS OF GOOD LEADERSHIP

Several experts describe the characteristics that are necessary for good leadership. A look at these sources reveals that there are overlaps among various of the characteristics identified. Good leadership has also been associated with respect, honesty, integrity, empathy, dedication, accountability, vision, discipline, determination, persistence, initiative, positive thinking, as well as with care for others, emotional intelligence, fairness, and justice. Some think of transformational leaders as good leaders that possess many of the traits that are associated with good leadership. Courage, sense of responsibility, justice, openness, humanity, and the ability to earn the trust, respect and admiration of followers are seen as important and common factors that are associated with good leadership (Crossan, Gandz, & Seijts, January/February 2012; Jewett- Geragosian, 2018;Stauffer, March 19, 2020). The ability to be highly communicative, accountable, responsible, visionary, self-motivated, confident, people-oriented, and emotionally stable are other attributes that have been associated with good leadership (Corporate Finance Institute, 2021; Conant Leadership, July 26, 2017),and these are also qualities that are associated with transformational leadership. Good leaders are expected to have most of these skills as well as life skills, competencies, character skills and relevant job skills.

The Center for Creative Leadership (September 10, 2020) also describes characteristics of good leaders as including integrity, ability to delegate, communication, self-awareness, gratitude, learning ability, influence, empathy, courage and respect. But not all good leaders have all of these characteristics; but some characteristics are seen as essential. As pointed out, "While successful leaders may exhibit these 10 leadership skills to varying degrees, all good leaders leverage at least some – or most – of these characteristics" (Center for Creative Leadership, September 10, 2020).

IMPORTANCE OF LEADERSHIP FOR STUDENTS

One question that may be asked is "Why should students be so concerned with leadership at this point in their lives?" After all, students may consider themselves still quite young and just making up their minds as to what they want to do. Many students may not be thinking of going into business, politics, law, or other careers where formal leadership characteristics are important. So, why bother about leadership?

NECESSARY SKILLS FOR 21ST CENTURY STUDENTS

While these are characteristics and qualities that apply to professional leaders, they are also relevant to the development of leadership in students. Experts point out that the skills that 21st century students need should include leadership. These experts describe leadership as one of the life skills necessary for participating in the global economy. Soffel (March 10, 2016) at the World Economic Forum points out that 21st century skills for students must include foundational literacies, competencies, and character qualities. While the fundamental literacies identified include literacy, numeracy, scientific literacy, literacy in Information and Communication Technologies (ICT), financial literacy, cultural and civil literacy, competencies include critical thinking and problem solving, creativity, and communication and collaboration. However, all of these skills depend on 21st century students possessing character qualities, such as curiosity, initiative, persistence, adaptability, leadership and social and cultural awareness (Soffel, March 10, 2016). Leadership is therefore considered a critical character quality that students must have. Interestingly, a look at what constitute leadership skills for students overlap with the character qualities mentioned earlier as belonging to successful leaders.

PEOPLE OF ANY AGE COULD BE LEADERS

In response to the earlier question of why students should be concerned about leadership, the answer is straightforward. Leadership is a role that people, regardless of age, are often called upon to perform, even if they do not have a job as a leader. Mark Sanborn in a famous quote pointed out, "You don't need a title to be a leader". Similarly, Henry Ford, reportedly observed, "You don't have to hold a position in order to be a leader." A call to leadership can take place within the family, in emergency situations, at work, in a group, in a class, or among friends. In order to equip themselves for adulthood, young people need to explore the various roles that they would be called upon to perform from time to time. The more frequently they consider some of these roles, the more prepared they would be to perform these roles when called upon to do so.

YOUNG PEOPLE TAKING INITIATIVES

While the role of leader may be something that a young person is called upon to perform in an emergency situation, at times the role of leader is something that a young person may consider out of a sense of duty. An individual may feel very strongly about doing something to promote the wellbeing of his/her community. In situations like these, such an individual may feel compelled to play this leadership role. Mother Teresa explains the wisdom of this call to leadership when she noted, "I alone cannot change the world, but I can cast a stone across the water to create many ripples." Being a leader could involve creating "ripples" that could attract followers to bring about great change. An individual may recognize that if something is to get done, he/she needs to take responsibility for doing it or at least shining a light on what needs to be done. In cases like these, an individual takes the initiative and proves to be a leader.

MANY OPPORTUNITIES FOR LEADING

There are many opportunities for leading. Opportunities could occur in your home, school and community, where you demonstrate the qualities of leadership examined in this book for successful living. You can also participate in larger enterprises where you can use the same leadership qualities that you develop in your personal life in influencing change in larger contexts. Following are examples of how young people are doing great things in improving themselves, their communities, and the world at large. The areas that are highlighted are the environment and social justice in general.

FOR THE ENVIRONMENT – THE UNITED NATIONS

In recent years, many young people have taken on leadership roles in calling attention to measures for improving the environment. Organizations are also recognizing this and are supporting the work of young people. The United Nations (UN) is promoting local entrepreneurship by declaring 2021 to 2030 as the DECADE OF ECOSYSTEM RESTORATION, and is encouraging commitment and action through partnerships between the young and old in service of promoting restoration of the environment (Kaiser, January 28, 2021).

GLOBAL FOREST GENERATION – ONE EXAMPLE

For example, on a global scale, some young people have linked the economy with environmental health. As Florent Kaiser, Executive Director of Global Forest Generation, observed: "Sparked by a formidable sense of purpose, urgency and need for action, a new generation of young people are putting the planet's healing at the heart of their business." Global Forest Generations is a youth-led movement that is an example of how local grassroots restoration (young) leaders are joining with rural and Indigenous communities to protect 1 million hectares of land while growing 1 million trees to replace those trees that had been removed over time. This movement involves young people working with seniors to achieve this goal. Global Forest Generation is made up of several smaller local grassroots organizations in the Andes of South America, all aimed at restoring the environment, and is part of the UN agency endeavour.

FOR THE ENVIRONMENT – WORLD ECONOMIC FORUM

The World Economic Forum (WEF) through its 1t. org supports this UN agenda and so is bringing together world leaders, businesses, as well as young entrepreneurs, who could work together to promote and support this agenda. The 1t. org has a very large environmental agenda as it has set out to accomplish as its goal that of "conserving, restoring and growing 1 trillion trees by 2020" (Kaiser, January 28, 2021). The emphasis is on 'growing' rather than 'planting' trees, for implicit in this distinction is that 'growing' implies taking responsibility to ensure that the trees that are planted are nurtured into maturity.

WEF through its 1t. org program presently has hubs in the United States, Sahel, the Amazon Basin and India, and through its UpLink Trillion Trees Challenges and Accelerator programs helps promising innovations to scale up. The Corporate Alliance that is part of the 1t. org initiative engages companies that are committed to conservation, restoration and reforestation and that are willing to provide help and support.

This is a worthwhile cause in which young people and older ones are encouraged to participate to find an answer to the climate change problem that is ravaging all parts of the world today. This initiative also boasts an ample library that produces ideas as well as helpful lessons on how individuals, countries, corporations and organizations can participate.

FOR SOCIAL JUSTICE

Also, in recent years, many young people have taken on leadership roles in calling attention to and exposing social injustices in human rights, equality rights and civil rights. Young people and not-so-young people have been peacefully protesting violations of these rights around the world. Several organizations such as Black Lives Matter, Amnesty International, Anti-Slavery International, Centre for Economic and Social Rights, Human Rights Watch, Civil Rights Defenders, Physicians for Human Rights, and numerous human rights organizations have raised global awareness of social injustices. They have spotlighted the effects of social injustice caused by racial disparities and violations of human rights against Blacks, Latinx, Indigenous, LBGTQA+, minority ethnic, religious and other marginalized groups in the United States and in other nations. Organizations such as these have raised the consciousness of many people around the world to recognize the importance of seeing every individual as worthy of respect and human dignity.

A HOPE FOR NOW

Maybe with this greater global awareness among young people in 2019, 2020, and 2021, in wake of the great injustices that have been perpetrated against innocent people the world over, and the realization with the experience of COVID-19 that no one is above the human condition, it is time for action. National governments, corporate entities, community organizations, social justice and international organizations like the United Nations and the World Economic Forum can all come together to declare 2021 to 2030 the DECADE OF HUMAN RIGHTS RESTORATION.

Wouldn't this be a fitting complement to the declaration of DECADE OF ECOSYSTEM RESTORATION?

JUST IMAGINE!

Just imagine what could be accomplished if individuals of all races, classes, and differences, nations of all political stripes, corporations of all sizes, community, social justice and international organizations recognize the need and decide to seriously work together to not only save our environment, our Planet Earth, but also to restore human dignity and respect to all people!It may seem difficult and far-fetched to envision, but much could happen within the space of a year and surely within the space of a decade.

Just think of the ravages of the pandemic and the loss of over 2. 5 million of Planet Earth's people within a year!!But also think of the great strides that were made as nations, scientists, and organizations came together to create vaccines in just over a year, a feat that before this usually took years to become a reality.

What this says is that if we see ourselves as one people, as humans, striving for our common survival, that we could accomplish great things working together.

With thoughtful, committed and global leadership, great accomplishments could be made in healing the planet and its people, regardless of where we live and who we are.

CHAPTER 29 - FOOD FOR THOUGHT – LEADERSHIP IN PERSPECTIVE

TOPICS AND IDEAS FOR SELF-REFLECTION AND DISCUSSION

SELF-REFLECTION

"Watch your thoughts; they become words. Watch your words; they become actions. Watch your actions; they become habits. Watch your habits; they become character. Watch your character; it becomes your destiny." Frank Outlaw

Think about this definition of a leader's role:

"A leader's role is to raise people's aspirations for what they can become and to release their energies so they will try to get there." David Gergen

GROUP DISCUSSION

Discuss in your group or write about the quote by Peter F. Drucker.

"Leadership is not magnetic personality, that can just as well be a glib tongue. It is not 'making friends and influencing people,' that is flattery. Leadership is lifting a person's vision to higher sights, the raising of a person's performance to a higher standard, the building of a personality beyond its normal limitations." --Peter F. Drucker

While Peter Drucker was speaking about leaders within the formal organization, his advice could be applied to an informal setting. If one can influence others to perform better and become outstanding individuals, one is a leader. What do you think?

Discuss in your group or write about this quote by Nelson Mandela.

"A leader is like a shepherd. He stays behind the flock, letting the most nimble go out ahead, whereupon the others follow, not realizing that all along they are being directed from behind." Nelson Mandela

Some have spurned the idea of "leading from behind" and see this as weakness or as an abnegation of leadership. But the truth is, what is important is that one is playing a leading role in helping to make something great happen. One does not have to be out front, looking for credit, fame, money, or acknowledgement. Getting the job done is what leadership is about? What do you think?

How can you and/or your group play a leadership role in promoting social justice in your community?

CHAPTER 29 – REFERENCES AND FURTHER READING

Arenas, F. J. , Connelly, D. & Williams, M. D. (2017). *Developing Your Full range Leadership: Leveraging a Transformational Approach*, (11-36). The Full Range Leadership Model. Air University Press.

Center for Creative Leadership (September 10, 2020) 10 characteristics of a good leader. Available at *https://www. ccl. org/blog/characteristics-good-leader*

Colbert, A. E. , Judge, T. A. , Choi, T. A. & Wang, G. (2012). Assessing the trait theory of leadership, using self and observer ratings of personality: The mediating role of contribution to group success. *The Leadership Quarterly, 23*(4), 670-685.

Conant Leadership (July 26, 2017). Why taking responsibility is always the best leadership choice. Inspire Trust. Available at *https://conantleadership. com/why-taking-responsibility-best-leadership-choice/*

Corporate Finance Institute (2021). What are leadership traits? Available at *https://corporatefinanceinstitute. com/resources/careers/soft-skills/leadership-traits-list/*

Crossan, M, Gandz, J. & Seijts, G. (January/February 2012). Developing leadership character. *Ivey Business Journal*. Available at https://iveybusinessjournal. com/publication/developing-leadership-character

Driscoll, M. (February 15, 2016). School leadership for the 21st century. Retrieved from *https://thinkstrategicforschools. com/leadership-in-schools/*

Ebenezer-Abiola, R. and Moore, J. *What Works in Youth Projects: Lessons for the Youth, Peace, and Security Field.* US Institute of Peace, 2020

Eva, N. , Robin, M. , Sendjaya, S. van Dierendonck, S. & Liden, R. C. (2019). Servant leadership: A systematic review and call for future research. *The Leadership Journal, 30*(1), 111-132.

Forbes Coaches Council (January 27, 2021). 14 Ways to prepare for how Gen Z will impact the workforce. Forbes. Available at *https://www. forbes. com/sites/forbescoachescouncil/2021/01/27/14-ways-to-prepare-for-how-gen-z-will-impact-the-workforce/?sh=70b7835c2b77*

Fuller, R. C. , Harrison, C. K. , Bukstein, S. , Martin, B. E. , Lawerence, M. & Parks, C. (Winter 2017). The Impact of High School on the Leadership Development of African American Male Scholar-Athletes . *The High School Journal,* Vol. 100, No. 2 (Winter 2017), pp. 146-162

Goertzen, B. J. *Contemporary Theories of Leadership.* Jones & Bartlett Learning.

House, R. J. & Howell, J. M. (1992). Personality and charismatic leadership. *The Leadership Quarterly, 3*(2), 81-108.

Jewett-Geragosian, R. (2018). Styles and Traits Theory. Chapter 7: Theories of effective leadership include trait, contingency, behavioral, and full-range theories. Granite College Press. Available at *https://granite. pressbooks. pub/ld820/chapter/7/*

Kaiser, F. (January 28, 2021). The rise of Generation Restoration and young ecopreneurship. World Economic Forum. Available at *https://www. weforum. org/agenda/2021/01/the-rise-of-generation-restoration-and-youth-ecopreneurship/*

Khan, M. S. , Khan, I. , Qureshi, Q. A. , Ismail, H. M. , Rauf, H. et al. (2015). The Styles of Leadership: A Critical Review. *Public Policy and Administration Research, 5(3)*, 87-92.

Kuhnert, K. , & Lewis, P. (1987). Transactional and Transformational Leadership: A Constructive/Developmental Analysis. *The Academy of Management Review, 12(4)*, 648-657.

Lalonde, J. M. (May 9, 2018). How leadership is a relationship. Available at *https://www. jmlalonde. com/how-leadership-is-a-relationship/*

Mitra, D. L. (2009). Collaborating with students: Building youth-adult partnerships in schools. *American Journal of Education, 115(3)*, 407-436.

Morgan, J. (January 6, 2020). What is leadership and who is a leader. Available at *https://www. chieflearningofficer. com/2020/01/06/what-is-leadership-and-who-is-a-leader/*

Quinn, J. (1999). When Need Meets Opportunity: Youth Development Programs for early teens. When School is Out. *The Future of Children, 9(2)*, 96-116

Rafaeil, J. (Spring) 2020). The Leaders of Tomorrow are shaped by the volunteers of today. *Women of Color Magazine, 20*(1), 14-15.

Rowold, J. (2014). Instrumental leadership: Extending the transformational-transactional leadership paradigm. *Zeitschrift Für Personal for schung/German Journal of Research in Human Resource Management, 28*(3), 367-390.

Shockness, I. (2020). *Respect is Only Human: A Response to Disrespect and Implicit Bias.* Vanquest Publishing.

Soffel, J. (March 10, 2016). What are the 21st-century skills every student needs? World Economic Forum. Available at *https://www. weforum. org/agenda/2016/03/21st-century-skills-future-jobs-students/*

Stauffer, B. (March 19, 2020). What are 21st century skills? Available at *https://www. aeseducation. com/blog/what-are-21st-century-skills*

Sutton, S. E. (2007). A Social Justice Perspective on Youth and Community Development: Theorizing the Processes and Outcomes of Participation. *Children, Youth and Environments, 17*(2), 616-645.

World Economic Forum 1t. org (n. d.). A platform for the trillion tree community. Available at *https://www. 1t. org/*

CHAPTER 30

CONCLUSION: MAKING THIS BOOK WORK FOR YOU

DEMONSTRATING LEADERSHIP

Now that you are at the end of this book, it is my hope that you have considered some of the topics discussed and have explored views that may have been different from yours. Remember, you do not have to agree with everything, but at least you have taken the time to consider how you feel about the ideas and the situations presented. Remember also, this is an opportunity for you to use critical thinking.

Whether you are a teen or young adult, I encourage you to share some of these ideas with friends, family members, and peers. Fireside or online chats, dinner conversations, recess chatter, watercooler talk, and classroom discussions are all opportunities for sharing. The opening up of these talks to a friend could be simply, "I was reading a book today and it got me thinking about being a really good leader when I am just an ordinary person. What do you think about this?" You may add, "I have the book, in case you want a read." Be comfortable with your talk. One thing may lead to another and before you know it, you may be having a vibrant conversation on the subject of how to develop leadership qualities. Or you may also find that because you raise the subject, the person you are speaking to feels comfortable enough with you to talk about some difficult issue he or she may be experiencing. This may be the opportunity this person may have been wishing for to start a conversation and get help. You may just have opened the channels of communication with your friend or peer.

If you are a parent or an older adult, introduce this book to young people, allowing them to consider some of the situations and possible opportunities highlighted. If you are a teacher, a youth group leader, or someone who works with young people, encourage discussion and promote critical thinking among them. Just giving a young person a copy of the book may be all you may need to do to get a conversation started. Or maybe, there will be no talk, but the person may read the book.

The objective here is only to get young people engaging with the subjects discussed and allowing them the opportunity to share ideas with peers and others. It is a further hope that this book encourages more open discussion on a host of issues that may have nothing to do with leadership.

I firmly believe that we sometimes take it for granted that regardless of our ages we have common knowledge about things. But this is not often the case with young people, who may not have had the vast life experiences that many adults have had. Consequently, they are unaware of some of the pitfalls that we all have to face. Not all older people share common ideas on many of these issues. However, addressing some issues as topics for discussion before having to face them in real life could go a long way to alleviating some of the stress - emotional and mental health -that many young people experience and which they try to deal with in silence.

By sharing with others, young people have the opportunity to make their own decisions. By agreeing or disagreeing with ideas and using critical thinking, many young people are able to think more clearly and decide more convincingly on important issues for themselves.

I would welcome hearing about your experiences with these topics and would appreciate your feedback, which I would use to improve this book. I can be reached at info@SuccessfulYouthLiving. com. Thanks.

MORE READING AVAILABLE

If you found this book beneficial, you may also want to consider trying out some of the other books in this series. See the back of the book for details. You may also want to send us comments to info@IsraelinShockness. com.

"Thanks for reading! If you found this book useful, please post a short review where you obtained this book. I read all the reviews personally so I can get your feedback and make this book even better.